The Freedom Path

Formerly "Your Mind Net"

by

Robert E. Detzler

Edited by

Elizabeth Grobes

SRC Publishing

Redmond, Washington

The case studies in this book have been taken from actual counseling sessions and seminars. The names of the clients and students involved have been changed to protect their privacy.

The Freedom Path reflects the views and personal experience of the author. No medical claim is made as to the effect or outcome of the exercises described in this volume. Each person is encouraged to be responsible in the use and choice of professional healing assistance as needed.

Library of Congress Cataloging-in-Publication Data

Detzler, Robert E.

The freedom path, your mind net to clear your soul records / by Robert Ernest Detzler. Second edition

Includes bibliographical references, glossary of terms.

1. Spiritual healing, case studies.

2. Self actualization (Psychology—Miscellanea.)

3. Extrasensory perception. I. Title

ISBN 0-9640041-2-7: $15.95

1996 Library of Congress Catalog Number 96-067786

Cover design and illustrations by Philip Brautigam Design

Edited by Elizabeth Grobes

Published in the United States of America by SRC Publishing

Printed in the United States of America by
Snohomish Publishing Company, Inc., Snohomish, Washington

Dedication

I dedicate this book to the High Self. The High Self is a group of spiritual beings who Jesus referred to as the Father within. This group has led me step by step to each new awareness necessary to gather and present this material. I could not have brought this book forth by myself. The High Self has revealed to me through dreams, inspiration, and many clients (who have been my teachers) a constantly expanding knowledge of how the puzzle of life fits together.

I do not honestly feel that I have written this book, but that I have simply allowed the material to pour through me as it was given by my High Self.

Acknowledgments

I especially appreciate and thank the following persons for their contribution to the material of this book: Dr. Clark Cameron who taught me the first eight program types used in Response Therapy; Elizabeth Grobes, editor; Phyllis Brewer, who showed me how to set up the first chart which saved a lot of time in the process of Spiritual Response Therapy; Mary Marie Satterlee, who taught me how to work with my High Self and how to free discarnates; my wife, Mary Ann, who gave me encouragement and valuable suggestions; all of the many clients, who gave me permission to use their examples; Jerry Young and Don Depue, who taught me how to use a computer; and to my High Self, who taught me patience and many other lessons.

Preface

The first edition of this book was entitled, *Your Mind Net.* All the topics and case studies included in *Your Mind Net* have been retained in this second edition, titled: *The Freedom Path.* However, we have greatly revised the order in which the material is presented. We have also included new material and revised the techniques in accordance with our current understanding and procedures.

THIS METHOD OF SPIRITUAL COUNSELING IS NOT MEANT TO BE A SUBSTITUTE FOR PROFESSIONAL MEDICAL CARE OR PSYCHOLOGICAL COUNSELING.

Contents

Figures

CHAPTER 1

Introduction
ဆ ထ

What is The "Mind Net?"

The conscious mind is like a net. It gathers information through the senses and forms ideas, beliefs and judgments and stores them in the subconscious mind. Every thing you have observed through your senses and all the thoughts and feelings you have experienced as a result of those observations are stored in the subconscious mind below the surface of your awareness.

As children, before we have fully developed our ability to reason and discriminate, we often store erroneous beliefs, perceptions and judgments. So, too, in the years before we begin our spiritual journey, and even in the early years of that journey, we may have experiences or are exposed to ideas which may cause pain and confusion. We may blame and feel victimized instead of taking responsibility for what we create. Even today, we may not always express our best selves. We may feel anger, fear, guilt, etc. All is stored in the subconscious mind. You can liken this process to a computer and the programs which are stored in it.

Unlike the non-discriminating, accepting subconscious mind, the conscious mind is objective and has the ability to observe, to use logic and to discriminate. As a spiritually-aware adult, you can use the conscious mind to sort through the contents of the subconscious mind and release the destructive ideas and feelings. In their place, you plant positive ideas and feelings of love and peace.

This on-going process of mind purification (or re-programming) gradually changes the balance of supportive and limiting ideas held in the subconscious mind. As the content of your subconscious mind becomes more supportive and loving, these positive ideas will create a more positive life experience. You will draw to yourself a fuller experience of good.

This process of mind purification, this Freedom Path, is called Spiritual Response Therapy (SRT). With SRT, we can not only research and clear the subconscious mind, but also the entire soul record.

The Soul (Akashic) Record

The soul record is commonly referred to as the Akashic Record. It is the record of everything the soul has experienced from the instant that the Divine Blueprint was formed at the level of the GODHEAD until the present moment and beyond. All the programming from this and other lives is stored there.

What is Spiritual Response Therapy (SRT)?

SRT is a system of researching the subconscious mind and soul records to quickly find and release the discordant, limiting ideas and replace them with loving, supportive ideas and beliefs. SRT provides an exacting, powerful, virtually painless and accurate way of changing the landscape of our inner and outer lives. Thus, SRT enables us to live our lives more freely.

The system of SRT involves the use of a pendulum, a set of charts, and a specific series of questions to complete the research and clearing of all discordant programming in the subconscious mind and soul record.

Development of SRT

In 1986, I studied with Dr. Clark and Sharon Cameron a system they called Response Therapy in which we used a pendulum to ask questions of our subconscious minds regarding blocks to a happy, fulfilled life experience. Dr. Cameron had adapted research by David B. Cheek, M.D., and Leslie M. LeCron, B.A., who had used seven of the current thirteen major program types as aids in hypnotherapy. As a result of his own research, Dr. Cameron added one more program type.

After beginning to work with the system, I discovered five more program types and was guided to list them on fan-shaped charts so that they could be quickly identified. Since that time, Spirit has revealed to me much more information in regard to the Godhead, how Life works, the soul's design, our relationship with God, the incarnational cycle, etc. Spirit has provided even more detailed information on the blocks to our oneness with God and to physical, emotional, material and spiritual well-being and how to clear the blocks.

Due to the on-going nature of the development of SRT, The Spiritual Response Association publishes monthly newsletters and sponsors monthly meetings. Tapes and transcripts of the monthly meetings are available from the Association. It is through these avenues and through classes that the most recently received information is shared with students of SRT.

Much of the information Spirit has provided is now contained in two textbooks on SRT. *Your Mind Net* is the first book I wrote on the system we named Spiritual Response Therapy. *Your Mind Net* has now been changed to *The Freedom Path/Your Mind Net* and the second book is titled *Soul Re-Creation*.

Textbooks

This book, *The Freedom Path*, presents the basic concepts and techniques of SRT, case studies, and the biblical, psychological and scientific premises upon which Spiritual Response Therapy is founded. The advanced techniques, more case studies and further spiritual understandings are presented in the second volume, *Soul Re-Creation*. These books are required reading for the Basic and Advanced Spiritual Response Therapy training classes. These classes are taught throughout the U.S. and in foreign countries under the aegis of the Spiritual Response Association which certifies teachers and counselors of SRT.

This book presents a step-by-step process of working with the subconscious mind. Read the book through from cover to cover before you form any opinion or try working with the system. Then re-read it as you proceed with the actual work. Be certain you completely understand how to use it before you begin. Follow the system exactly as it is presented or you may find yourself in one confusing blind alley after another. Being aware of some of the problems you may encounter will save you a lot of frustration as you begin the actual clearing work.

CHAPTER 2

The Mind Net
ℰↃ ℭℛ

Again, the kingdom of heaven is like unto a net, that was cast into the sea, and gathered of every kind: Which, when it was full, they drew to shore, and sat down, and gathered the good into vessels, but cast the bad away. So shall it be at the end of the world: the angels shall come forth and sever the wicked from among the just and shall cast them into the furnace of fire: there shall be wailing and gnashing of teeth. (Matthew 13:47-50)†

The Parable of the Net

The "parable of the net," on the surface, suggests that Jesus is challenging people to change their sinful ways. A superficial interpretation is that people are going to be separated into two groups—the good and the wicked—and the wicked will be cast into a furnace of fire. This is not the intent of the parable at all. I believe that Jesus, the greatest psychologist of all time, was talking about the principles of how the mind works: How we may access the beliefs, perceptions and judgments that are in our subconscious mind, and clear them so that we may live life fully and freely.

The Parable of the Sower

To more fully understand what Jesus taught about the psychology of man's mind, let's take a look at the first parable that Jesus gave. This is often called the "parable of the sower."

And he spake many things unto them in parables, saying, Behold, a sower went forth to sow; And when he sowed, some seeds fell by the way side, and the fowls came and devoured them up: Some fell upon stony places, where they had not much earth: and forthwith they sprung up, because they had no deepness of earth: And when the sun was up, they were scorched; and because they had no root, they withered away. And some fell among thorns; and the thorns sprung up, and choked them: But other fell into good ground, and brought forth fruit, some an hundredfold, some sixtyfold, and some thirtyfold. Who hath ears to hear, let him hear. (Matthew 13:3-9)

After Jesus had presented His first parable, His disciples asked Him to interpret it for them and He gladly did so. (See Matthew 13:11-23.) He revealed that man was a being of consciousness to whom God was constantly sending forth His word. Or, you might say, God was constantly planting "seed ideas," in man's mind. When man's mind is open and receptive, the seed ideas grow and bring forth great good. When man is not receptive, but is caught up in the cares and fears of the world, the good seed does not take root and grow. So it is with everyone today, not only are we receiving ideas from God, we are constantly receiving ideas from the environment and from those with whom we associate. Our life, good or bad, is determined by the seed ideas we plant in the soil of our subconscious minds.

---

†All Bible references in this book are from the King James Version. The Holy Bible is the most misquoted, misinterpreted, misunderstood, and misused book that has ever been compiled. Not only has it been used as a club to mentally beat people over the head, but, because of a general misunderstanding of the very principles of the Scriptures, it has been used as a weapon of fear regarding what can happen to those who do not fully accept Holy Scriptures at their face value.

Man as a Being of Consciousness

Jesus, the great psychologist, fully understood the nature of man as a being of consciousness and used parables to present the principles by which man can direct his own life with wisdom and understanding. The basic premise of all of Jesus' parables is that we, as beings of consciousness, are constantly receiving impressions from Spirit. Thus the Holy Bible is a record of the unfolding of man as a being of consciousness—from the darkness of not knowing into the light of spiritual understanding. And only this spiritual understanding will set man free from the darkness of ignorance and despair.

With this in mind, the "parable of the net" takes on another significance. The "net" may be understood to be the conscious mind. The "sea" is the subconscious mind. "Every kind" (fish) are the ideas, beliefs and concepts which are swimming below the surface of the conscious mind. The "angels" are spiritual ideals or right thinking (inspiration of God) that help us recognize discordant thoughts and feelings and eliminate them—burn them up.

The conscious mind, like a net, gathers information through the senses and forms ideas, beliefs, perceptions, and judgments. It qualifies the information gathered, makes determinations, and directs the conscious affairs of the individual. The conscious mind is objective by nature and has the ability to observe, to use logic, and to discriminate. You might say it is the executive director of man's being. Unfortunately, when we are children, our conscious minds may accept many ideas into the subconscious mind before we have fully developed our abilities to reason and discriminate.

The subconscious mind, like the "sea," teems with every kind of idea and belief. Recorded there is every experience of sight, sound, taste, touch, smell, thought, and feeling. It contains all that you have observed through your five senses, as well as all the thoughts and feelings you have experienced as a result of those observations. These are the fish or ideas that are in the sea of the subconscious mind swimming below the surface of our awareness. They can be caught by the conscious mind and sorted. The good ideas (fish) can be retained and the bad ones, those that cause pain or confusion, can be cast into the furnace of fire—which simply means a process of purification.

God created humans as living souls, beings of consciousness. As a being of consciousness, you create your own world based on the information gathered by the five senses. When you are centered in a pure consciousness of good, you know that all experiences are part of the human growth process. You understand that every experience is a lesson. When you realize this, you can look for the lesson involved in each experience, learn from it, release the energy, and move on to the next lesson. This is what is meant by "keeping your eye single to the glory of God." It is finding the good in all that comes to you. Eventually, you will have released the destructive ideas from the subconscious and conscious minds and the good ideas (fish) gathered will then form a new world or outer projection.

As you walk this freedom path of mind purification, you begin to fill your mind with ideas of good and positive things begin to happen. It is therefore imperative that you stand guard at the doorway of your conscious mind and allow only the good beliefs to enter. When you do so, you gradually change the balance of good and evil in your "sea" (subconscious mind) and the outer expression of your life will improve in a positive way as the new beliefs begin to manifest themselves as your world. This can be a slow or fast process of purification depending on the amount of time and effort you are willing to invest.

This process of mind purification is not a one-time activity. It is, rather, a conscious awareness of the ideas being presented by the outside world and of the concepts coming from the subconscious mind. You can use your conscious discernment to sort through and select only the good ideas and beliefs and reject that which is not of the highest order. This will bring peace, freedom, joy, and satisfaction.

Although the subconscious mind holds many beliefs that can be limiting, or cause mental, emotional, and physical trauma, it also controls the complete functioning of the physical body through the autonomic nervous system. Once you have learned a skill such as walking, brushing your teeth, singing a song, dancing, etc., you do not have to relearn it each time you want to demonstrate it. You simply recall it from the subconscious mind through an automatic process and extend it into the outer expression in the appropriate manner. It is the same with behavior patterns.

There are times when most of us have asked ourselves, "What makes me act like that? Why can't I succeed at what I want to do? I wonder why nothing ever seems to work for me?" These and a myriad of other questions rise up to cause us to wonder, "What is wrong with me?" The answers to all of these questions and to many more lie in the depths of the subconscious mind. Every sight, sound, taste, touch, and smell as well as every thought and feeling your senses have experienced is recorded in the subconscious mind.

Anyone can sit quietly and call to mind, more or less clearly, scenes from the past, even from early childhood. With the aid of a hypnotist, even forgotten areas of the past can be brought to the awareness of the conscious mind and relived in detail. Emotions experienced at the time of the event can be re-experienced and even the words in a conversation can be re-called. Many people who have suppressed childhood memories that are causing current problems find great benefit in working with a hypnotist to expose old subconscious programs so they can deal with them. Sometimes, however, working with a hypnotist can stir up extremely painful memories and feelings and recreate the agony of the past. The hypnotist is aware of this possibility and is trained to reassure the client and move them through the experience quickly.

Hypnotism is only one way of researching the past in order to find and release mental and emotional blocks which may be seriously restricting the client's meaningful expression of life. Our knowledge of man's psyche is understood better today than ever before. This is the day of self-diagnosis, self-help and self-realization.

There are countless books written on the mind and how to change and reshape restrictive beliefs, release phobias, and achieve a new direction in life. There are many schools of thought on the subject and almost as many methods of dealing with human problems and of bringing about cures. There are new theories and new groups springing up overnight, all with the promise of a sudden release from the personal ills of the individual.

All are claiming to be the ultimate cure for the problems of the world. The last great frontier is not outer space but inner space, and despite the great advances in the study of the mind, there is more to learn, much, much more to learn. The mind and its functioning seems fathomless and the various schools of thought seldom agree on how to handle phobias, bring about a cure, and establish the well-being of the individual.

All these techniques have the disadvantage of taking many hours, sometimes years, to find the source of the difficulty. Besides, problem areas of life may be so deeply buried that they cannot be uncovered with traditional counseling techniques. While talking things out with a friend, a counselor, or in a group can lead to insights as to what is causing a problem and bring inspiration as to how to handle and change it; usually, for most people, talking about their problems just reinforces them and pushes them down deeper into the subconscious.

The Freedom Path—Spiritual Response Therapy

However, there is a Freedom Path. There is a mind "net" that you can use to catch these erroneous beliefs. Spiritual Response Therapy (or "SRT") offers an exact way to look at the contents of the subconscious mind and sort through them. It provides a way to keep what is good, positive and constructive and to quickly cast the rest away. And most importantly, this comprehensive method enables the user to keep guard over the subconscious "sea," programming the subconscious mind with positive statements and thereby maintaining a high degree of positive ideas flowing from within. SRT, introduced in this book, provides an exacting, powerful, virtually painless, and accurate way of changing inner programs.

As a minister, I have the opportunity to work with a lot of people who are crying out for help. Their lives are out of control. The problems are as diverse as a breakdown in relationships, an experience of poverty, or a life-threatening illness. The ailments—mental, emotional, physical, and spiritual—are myriad. However, there seems to be one basic cause for all of the expressions of life, whether you name them "good" or "bad," and that is the beliefs that have been established in the conscious and subconscious minds. Although many beliefs are hidden from view in the subconscious mind, and there is no awareness of their existence, they still project themselves into your life regardless of your awareness or lack of it, and often cause discordant, restrictive, and hurtful effects.

Spiritual Response Therapy is the most powerful method of counseling that I have ever experienced. It has dramatically changed my life and the lives of many others.

CHAPTER 3

The System
ℰꙘ Ꙙℰ

Know ye not that ye are the temple of God
and that the Spirit of God dwelleth in you?
(1 Cor. 3:16)

How wonderfully we are made! What a powerful Spirit dwells within us. Yet, despite this
indwelling Spirit, there are few people who live
a full, happy, satisfied life. Is not this Spirit of
God that dwells within us capable of orches-
trating the life of a human being in a manner
that is reflective of full health, happiness,
satisfaction and abundance? Yes, it is! Then
why doesn't it?

Spirit is not a dictator who would force you to
heaven. Spirit is a benevolent counselor, guide,
and sustainer of all life. Never are you coerced
into doing anything even if it is for your higher
good. What you do with your individual life is
up to you. You have simply been given the
talents, abilities, and tools to build the kind of
life structure you believe in. That is the key—
BELIEF!

You may consciously believe in something and
strive with all your might to bring that belief to
fruition. Yet time after time you may be sty-
mied because your subconscious mind may
hide strong beliefs that are adverse to the very
thing you are trying to create.

It is my experience, that if there is disagree-
ment between the conscious desires, held in
mind, and the subconscious programming, the
subconscious will win. The way to assure that
your conscious beliefs will produce the good
results you desire is to make certain that there
are no adverse beliefs in the subconscious
mind that can block or cancel out the good you
are trying to experience. This is the purpose of
Spiritual Response Therapy.

The Nature of the Subconscious Mind

The subconscious mind is a marvelous instrument—an unlimited and invaluable tool which
every person may program and use to produce
an unlimited quantity of good. Right now, even
as you are reading this book, it is directing
countless automatic functions of mind and
body most of which you are unaware of and
take for granted.

Once you give the subconscious mind a message, it never lets go of the memory until you
deliberately tell it to release it. I call it the
"great computer." Like an electronic computer,
it makes no decisions but only feeds back
according to the commands given it and the
programs that are built into it. It is programmed by the conscious mind through the
sensing mechanisms of the body and through
thought and feeling (emotion). Once programmed, the subconscious mind is very
zealous, powerful, and exact in what it repro-
duces in your body, mind, and affairs. Like a
personal computer, it unerringly fulfills the
programming given it.

One client told me her life was confused and
difficult. Sometimes things went well and at
other times her life seemed to be in disarray.
Using Spiritual Response Therapy, we found
that she had a subconscious message. This
message had been given to her by an adult
figure when she (the client) fell down a flight of
stairs at the age of nine months. The adult
made a statement of concern about possible
damage to the child's brain. This statement
registered in the subconscious mind of the
distraught child—not as a possibility, but as
actual brain damage. Of course, anyone knows
that a person with brain damage will not

exhibit a normal life. This woman's life exhibited evidence of a brain damage message in that sometimes her life worked and sometimes it did not. A check of the subconscious revealed that there was actually no physical brain damage.

We cleared the subconscious mind of the brain damage message and checked to make certain it was deleted. We then programmed in positive messages of perfect brain and perfect brain functioning and checked to see that the new message was accepted. Since that time, this client's life has dramatically changed. Not only is the change obvious to her, but many of her friends have remarked that she has become a completely different person.

The subconscious mind responds to the orders you give it. You can deliberately access the subconscious mind through Spiritual Response Therapy, remove old programs, and add new ones at will. Once an order is given, the inner mind will draw to it from the universe and activate all of the necessary elements needed to manifest the idea given. As you become aware of the power you have to restructure the messages contained in the subconscious mind, you may then give it orders that will produce consistent positive results.

When you were a child, you were presented with many ideas that you accepted without question or qualification. Many of these ideas are now outdated and no longer viable. Had you been an adult, with the power of discrimination, you probably would never have accepted these concepts to begin with. Additionally, many of the messages you received and accepted were not understood, so that much of what is in your inner mind is fallacious and irrational. This can be very damaging to you as an individual and to your expression of a balanced, orderly life.

It is commonly accepted in the circle of New Thought churches that, "Thoughts held in the conscious and subconscious mind produce after their kind." However, thoughts in the conscious mind "produce after their kind" ONLY if there are no adverse thoughts in the subconscious mind. If there are conflicting messages or beliefs in the inner mind, they must be overridden or cast out before meaningful progress can be made toward establishing the new thought and bringing forth the

desired result. Many people know that things just do not seem to work out in a positive way for them. But, few realize that there may be beliefs in the subconscious mind that are blocking their greater good.

High Self—The Father Within

As you learn to use SRT to clear your subconscious mind, you will become aware that you are no longer working with just your subconscious. As the negative patterns are cleared, an important channel of communication begins to open up: your connection to your High Self. While we are always receiving guidance and help from the spiritual realm, we are not always aware of it. SRT is one method of bringing yourself into close conscious contact with your own spiritual helpers.

Everyone has a High Self. Your High Self is both a part of you and a part of the All. It is not an extension of your physical self; indeed, it is you who are an extension of the spiritual realm! Your High Self may consist of from one to an infinite number of beings. These beings may be from many different spiritual levels. The higher in consciousness they are, the greater their ability and the more help they can provide to you.

As you grow in level of soul consciousness or spiritual wisdom and stature, the members of your High Self committee may change. My High Self has changed many times as I have progressed along my path. You will also find that you can clear your High Self committee members of negative programs, just as you clear yourself.

Using a pendulum is just one way to communicate with your High Self. My High Self also communicates with me through inner pictures, sounds, feelings, knowing, and occasionally, smell. Many times as I am doing past life research, they show me images from the past lives, and provide other direct information. When I say that Spirit provided me with the information, I am talking about my High Self.

Like many things, communicating with your High Self takes practice. For some people, it can be like learning a foreign language. For others, it is as natural as thought. As you become clearer using SRT, pay attention to your thoughts and intuition. The High Self also communicates with us through dreams while we are asleep, and through visions while we are in meditation or an altered state of consciousness.

The Ideomotor Response

You cannot simply ask a question of the subconscious and have it answer you through your voice. Fortunately, the subconscious mind is in charge of all the autonomic body functions, so you can have it answer through a body movement. This is called an *ideomotor response* and limits the form of your questions to ones that can be answered by "yes" or "no" or by pointing to text on a chart or diagram.

David B. Cheek, M.D., and Leslie M. LeCron, B.A., in their book, *Clinical Hypnotherapy*, point out that the ideomotor movement is one of the most valuable tools for locating hidden subconscious messages. I have found the method to be fast and accurate. I can learn more information in one session than I can learn in many hours of free association questioning with a client. Using Spiritual Response Therapy and the ideomotor response does not reinforce a discordant message. It clears the problem completely.

Ideomotor responses have been used in hypnotism for decades. They take many forms—automatic writing, finger lift, eye movements, and the pendulum. All are common hypnotic techniques for uncovering unconscious messages.

The *Dictionary of Hypnosis* defines the ideomotor signal as a "signal made by a subject in a hypnotic state. The signal usually assumes the form of small, repetitive movements, such as finger jerks. These movements serve as signs of protest or distress; if disregarded, they are likely only to increase in vigor." The pendulum method, developed by M. Chevreul, is sometimes referred to as the Chevreul Pendulum. The *Dictionary of Hypnosis* describes the "Chevreul Pendulum" as a "portable contraption originally designed by M. Chevreul involving a pendulum (a weight suspended by a string about 15 inches long) swaying over a white chart on which two lines are drawn at right angles. It is sometimes used to determine and increase the subject's suggestibility or one's power of concentration."

In *Techniques of Hypnotherapy*, Leslie M. LeCron specifically identifies the pendulum as a tool that may be used with or without hypnosis. This is a critical point. If the client is properly prepared and centered when using the pendulum, it can be used to identify information in the subconscious without hypnosis. Spiritual Response Therapy provides all of the in-depth probing of hypnotherapy without inducing a trance and without the client having to re-live all the pain and emotions of the experiences brought to conscious awareness.

Contradictions Between Verbal and Ideomotor Responses

When there are contradictions between verbal and ideomotor answers, Cheek has found that the ideomotor answers are more reliable. An experiment regarding the validity of the pendulum was presented in LeCron's book, *Self Hypnotism: the Technique and Its Use in Daily Living.*

A number of obstetricians and other physicians questioned 402 pregnant women regarding the sex of their unborn child. Three hundred and sixty (90%) correctly predicted the sex of the child, including three sets of twins, where the fact of their being twins and their sex were both stated correctly. Among the errors, most of the women predicted the sex as being the one for which they had a preference. Probably, wishful thinking entered and the replies were on a voluntary basis rather than unconsciously controlled.

If you are using this questioning technique with some other person, it is usually possible to tell if the movements are being made consciously or if they are involuntary. With the pendulum, the hand or fingers may not seem to move at all, or any movement will be very slight, although of course there is some movement of the hand or the pendulum would hang motionless. Sometimes the hand can be seen to move and the swing of the pendulum is more pronounced. Just relax and let it move, resting in the assurance that you are not deliberately moving your hand, it is simply moved by the subconscious or the High Self.

The Pendulum

A pendulum may be any instrument such as a ring, a fishing weight, a heavy button, etc. to which a string is tied. Make the string about six inches long. Hold the string between the thumb and index finger with the weight hanging down as a pendulum. The pendulum should be heavy enough to move easily but not so heavy that it causes a strain on the fingers.

Establishing Yes and No Responses

To establish the movements for yourself or to demonstrate the ideomotor response to a client, sit in a chair with arms on it or at a desk or table of the right height so your elbow rests on a stable surface and is comfortable. This allows free movement of the hand and forearm without putting undo strain on the upper arm and shoulder. Bend your elbow and hold your hand, with thumb and first two fingers touching, about eight inches in front of you so you can easily see what the movements are. Then ask a question with a known affirmative answer and the subconscious mind will move your fingers in the direction of a "yes" answer. I usually ask, "Is my name Robert?" My fingers quickly move in a forward and back motion, but the movement is so minute it is almost unseen. Thus, we use a pendulum to magnify this movement.

First, draw a circle on a piece of paper and bisect it with two straight lines at right angles to each other. It should look similar to the drawing in Figure 3-1. Place the drawing on a flat surface, and, with a relaxed hand, dangle the pendulum over the point of intersection of the two lines. Make sure your pendulum is a fairly light object that will swing easily.

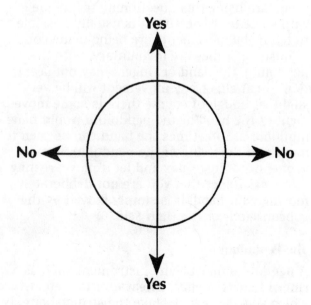

Figure 3-1. Establishing Yes and No Responses

Hold the pendulum up, and swing it forward and back while saying, "This is like nodding my head 'yes.' It is everyone's 'yes' and it will be my 'yes' also." Next, move it from side to side and say, "This is like shaking my head 'no.' It is everyone's 'no,' and will be my 'no' also." Repeat this procedure several times.

Next, hold the pendulum still and ask for a "yes," and then a "no" response. The pendulum should move in the appropriate direction for each question.

Blocks to Using a Pendulum

If you cannot get the pendulum to work for you consistently, you may have blocks to using a pendulum. These can be overcome. Use the instructions included in Chapter 8 to clear whatever may be keeping you from successfully using the pendulum.

Check Questions

After the standard "yes" and "no" responses have been determined, ask several questions with known "yes" and "no" answers to confirm that the responses have been firmly established.

One client's response to the confirming questions confused me. I asked if she were dancing at the Waldorf Astoria and her pendulum moved to indicate an immediate "yes" response. Since the Waldorf Astoria Hotel is in New York City and we were working in my office in California, I had expected a "no" response. Further questioning revealed that she had pictured herself dancing, and her subconscious mind had responded with an affirmative answer. The subconscious mind will answer according to what the conscious mind is asking or seeing. It does not differentiate between an actual happening and one that is created in the imagination. So be very specific in all your questioning. Now I ask, "Are you PHYSICALLY dancing at the Waldorf Astoria?"

Ideomotor Response Alternatives

If for some reason you are physically unable to use a pendulum, you can train your subconscious mind to use another ideomotor response such as an eye blink or head nod. For example, my subconscious will also answer "yes" with a single eye blink, and "no" with a double eye blink.

Teaching a Client to Use a Pendulum

When counseling others, I often teach my clients to use a pendulum so that they can participate in the research and clearing work. I then tell them what questions to ask so that they can receive the response directly. This not only helps them believe the answers, it empowers and encourages them to work directly with the subconscious, and eventually, the High Self.

Use the procedure explained above to teach a client how to use a pendulum. Then, have the client think of the question being asked of their subconscious and repeat the question quietly but firmly until an answer is received. Caution them not to let their mind stray to other questions. Have the person repeat the question silently not orally because some people cannot speak audibly without strong body movements that disrupt the movement of the pendulum. Once the responses are verified as being consistent, you are ready to start work clearing the subconscious mind.

While working with a client, occasionally use one or more check questions to make certain the responses received during the work process are correct. The question may be, "Are you swimming at the beach right now?" for a "no" answer, and, "Are you sitting in a chair in this office?" for a "yes" answer. Any questions with obvious answers will do.

My clients are usually amazed at how fast the pendulum moves when a question is asked of the subconscious mind. One woman was quite skeptical of using a pendulum. Soon after we started with Spiritual Response Therapy she said, "I know I am not moving this by my conscious mind, I can't think that fast. Before the message can go from my mind to my fingers, the pendulum is already moving."

One of the ways I sometimes use to show the client that it is the subconscious mind moving the pendulum and not their conscious mind, is to have them hold the pendulum still, after the "yes" and "no" responses have been established. I then ask several questions in my mind without voicing them and the client's pendulum will move in a "yes" or "no" direction according to the questions asked. I even close my eyes while asking the questions. When they are told the questions asked, they are amazed that the responses were correct.

Blocks to Working with SRT

Many people have programs that block them and keep them from working with SRT. If you are already working with SRT, you may have a blocking program, and may not be getting consistent, correct answers. When this happens, you could need the help of someone trained in the work to help you discover and clear the blocks. The trained counselor is able to work with his or her High Self in order to research the client's blocking program and clear it.

If you are just starting to learn SRT and find that you are getting confusing or inconsistent answers, ask your High Self if you can research and clear any blocks to working with the system by yourself before you call for help from another person. Every time I begin to do work for myself or anyone else, I always check to make certain I am not running a program and that I do not have blocks to getting correct answers.

First, I spend a few minutes centering myself through prayer. Then I ask if I am clear to work for myself or another person. As often as not, I have blocking energy that must be cleared before I can work. When I am unable to clear the blocks, I call on my wife or daughter for assistance. Both of them are trained in SRT.

There are many sources of blocks to using SRT. It could be from a past life experience, a negative childhood message which left a strong imprint in your subconscious or it could be from someone in spirit—a deceased relative or other soul who has not left the earth plane. Many of the blocks are listed on Chart 1. Blocks and Interference, but blocks can be found on all four charts. Chapters 8 and 21 contain definitions of all the items listed on Chart 1. Refer to Chapter 8 for in-depth instructions on how to remove blocks and interference to using SRT.

How to Use the Charts

The fan-shaped charts included in Appendix A of this book comprise the remainder of the tools you need to practice SRT. These charts make it easy for you to identify a wide range of programs that are blocking you or a client.

To use a chart, place the chart on a flat surface. Then place your elbow on the surface and dangle the pendulum over the circle located in the center of the "fan." When you ask a research question (as explained in Chapter 7), your subconscious, and later your High Self, provides an answer by swinging the pendulum in the direction of a particular word or phrase printed on the chart.

The remaining chapters of this book define the blocks and programs listed on the charts and show, via the case studies of clients who have had these blocks and programs, how to use the charts and clear the programs.

For information about:	See:
Chart 1	Chapter 8
Chart 2	Chapters 4 and 8 through 20
Chart 3	Chapter 5
Chart 4	Chapter 6

Figure 3-2. Where to Find Information About The Charts

Releasing Statements†

In Response Therapy, as I learned it from Clark and Sharon Cameron, we used a type of "affirmations and denials" called "releasing statements" to clear blocks and programs. Later, after I learned to work with my High Self, it was no longer necessary to use releasing statements because High Self can clear the programs. All we have to do is ask. However, there are still times when releasing statements can be beneficial.

Each person's individual expression of life is based on the beliefs that they hold in mind and the emotional energy that moves that belief slowly or quickly into action. The more emotionally charged a belief is the more quickly it manifests itself. Anger may explode into violent action, while fear may cause a person to tremble, withdraw within themselves, or run away. When you combine your thoughts with emotions, they become very powerful. "As a man thinketh in his heart, so is he..." states Proverbs 23:7.

The mind is the center of your thoughts and the heart is the center of your emotions. Because of your beliefs and perceptions and the energy charge you place on those beliefs and perceptions, you are constantly bringing various results into your mind, body, and affairs. In other words, you are receiving judgments. The Bible states, "Judge not, that ye be not judged. For with what judgment ye judge, ye shall be judged: and with what measure ye mete, it shall be measured to you again" (Matthew 7:1,2). "Judging is not only the act of judging but the result of judging" *(The Reader's Digest Great Encyclopedic Dictionary).*

As a being of consciousness you look at life through your five senses—sight, sound, taste, touch, and smell. You qualify what you perceive according to your beliefs and you get a result or judgment. For example, if I look out my office window, across the street I can see a tall object. It has a brown trunk which is rooted in the ground. Many branches grow from the trunk and they are covered with green needles. These branches are presently tossing in the wind. It is a pine tree or at least that is the belief I have according to the information given to me by others as I was growing up. I have thus used my beliefs to qualify what I have perceived and I now have a final result or judgment—a pine tree. So it is with programs. We qualify our perceptions with our beliefs to create judgments. Programs are nothing more, or less, than beliefs, perceptions and judgments. Releasing statements always follow a set format which is based on this fact.

There are three statements which must be said or written in a specific order.

The First Releasing Statement

When you are releasing programs, the first statement you will make begins: "I now release all my beliefs, perceptions, and judgments that..." Follow these words with a statement about what you wish to release.

Certainly, I could look out my window and say, "I release my belief, perception and judgment that is a pine tree." But such a statement is not going to change a thing in the outer world or in my conscious or subconscious mind, nor would

---

†Since all the case studies included in this book were from the very early days of my counseling practice using Spiritual Response Therapy, releasing statements are often referred to and even stated in the text. Because of the beneficial nature of releasing statements, we have chosen to retain all original references to releasing statements in this revised edition of *Your Mind Net*.

it serve any meaningful purpose to try to change such a belief. It is a pine tree. It is a current phenomenon and one that is easily observed and confirmed.

Neither would there be any benefit forthcoming from a statement that the woman who gave you birth was not your mother. All of the statements to the contrary would not change the relationship of mother and child. In fact, vehemently denying your mother would merely bind you closer to her with a discordant energy that could eventually prove destructive and cause you mental, emotional, or physical pain.

You can, however, release your beliefs, perceptions, and judgments regarding what a person has or has not done to you, because, what has been done is only a memory in the subconscious mind that may be recalled by the conscious mind. Since it is only a message recorded in the subconscious mind, it may be erased. Actually, it is more like defusing it or removing the potentially explosive charge of discordant energy. The awareness may still be in the conscious mind, but the mind is at peace because there is no longer any emotional charge attached to it.

Example: "I now release all belief, perception and judgment that my Mother and Father did not provide sufficient emotional and financial support while I was growing up." With such a statement, you are choosing to let go of the energy you hold on the judgment of "insufficient." Certainly, if you are able to function well enough to read this book, your parents provided a sufficient amount of emotional and financial support to get you this far. It may not have been enough to help you graduate from a university or realize some other dreams, but you are alive and able to help yourself. Such a statement allows you to let go of the negative energy and be at peace with your parents.

The Second Releasing Statement†

Once a belief system has been established there is a bulldog-like tendency to maintain it at all costs even if it is hurtful. Therefore, a second releasing statement is needed to clear this tendency.

The second statement you will make always begins: "I now release all need and desire to believe that..." Follow these words with the same statement with which you completed the first releasing statement. To carry our previous example a little further: "I now release all need and desire to believe that my Mother and Father did not provide sufficient emotional and financial support while I was growing up."

These two releasing statements are extremely effective in releasing old discordantly charged patterns from the subconscious mind.

The Reprogramming Statement

After these two statements are used to clear a program, you put in a new positive statement to replace the old discordant one. This statement begins: "I now completely accept and believe and I instruct my subconscious mind to completely accept and believe on every level of my being that..." Complete this statement with the ideal or preferred scenario or condition.

The example we have been using could be completed with this statement: "I now completely accept and believe and I instruct my subconscious mind to completely accept and believe on every level of my being that my parents did provide me with sufficient emotional and financial support while I was growing up." Or, a longer statement could be used which further describes your preferred appraisal of or feelings about your parents: "...They loved me and supported me in every way..." Or, you could add statements of truth as you know it: "There is only God. Therefore, there is only love. Therefore, my parents loved me and I love my parents."

The whole process is similar to turning on a computer, accessing a program, and giving the order to delete all or any part of it you choose. With a computer, you would see the words you had accessed appear on the screen and see them disappear when the proper commands are given. Unfortunately, the mind-computer does not have a screen on which to display the programs, so you simply use your hand-held pendulum and ask a check question to make certain the old program is deleted and the new program is in place.

---

†Since High Self can clear all programs, releasing statements are not necessary, but they can be of great benefit in certain situations, as explained in Chapter 3.

Unless a new program is desired, the electronic computer does not need to have a replacement message inserted after the erasure has been completed. However, when the subconscious mind is cleared, it is important to replace the old message with a new positive message. This helps the conscious mind accept that the old programs are gone and the new ones are in their place; and your life, from that point forward, will be created by the new positive programming.

Case study #1: Punishing self for incarnating

Mary Jane sat in my office in what appeared to be a total state of anxiety, verging on panic. The first program I discovered was self-punishment, which was established in past lives. In the past life we researched, she was Light. God and a Light Council of Nine were involved. Mary Jane was planning to incarnate for the first time. When I asked her questions to determine if all of them were in agreement about her incarnating, she received "yes" responses. This left me rather nonplused. I expected to find that either, or both, God and the Light Council were adverse to her incarnating. Then the reason for self-punishment would have been disobedience, or rebellion against God or the Council. "Spirit, I don't understand," I said. "What is going on? Why is she punishing herself?" I heard the words "dumb" and "stupid." I asked Mary Jane if she was punishing herself for incarnating because it was a dumb, stupid thing to do, and received a "yes" response. That was the only reason for self-punishment.

Mary Jane also had a program of panic. (See Chart 4.) She had been a Guardian Angel in charge of making Guardian Angel assignments and believed she had fouled up. She was in a panic, believing that God was going to get her for being so dumb and stupid.

Mary Jane, based on her perceptions and beliefs, had judged herself to be dumb and stupid because she left the realms of Light and incarnated. We used releasing statements to alter the inner perceptions and beliefs that she had recorded in her subconscious computer, and which had become the judgments causing her anxiety in the current life. Here are the statements I had her repeat.

"I release all belief, perception and judgment that it was a dumb, stupid thing to leave the realms of Light and incarnate."

"I release all need and desire to believe that it was a dumb, stupid thing to leave the realms of Light and incarnate."

"I now completely accept and believe and I instruct my subconscious mind to completely accept and believe on every level of my being that it was a wise and wonderful thing I did when I chose to incarnate for I have gained knowledge, wisdom, and stature in the sight of God."

We used the same type of releasing and reprogramming statements to remove the belief that she had fouled up as a Guardian Angel, and to establish a new sense of having done exactly right as a Guardian Angel. It worked! When Mary Jane left my office, she was completely at peace.

Sometimes clients or students question that they can clear something by affirming that it did not happen, because to do so would be a lie. I assure them that, according to Eastern teachings, everything is *Maya*, or illusion. Therefore, we are simply removing a discordant, limiting, or potentially destructive illusion and replacing it with a positive, constructive illusion. As the Scriptures state, "Death and life are in the power of the tongue, and those who love it will eat its fruits." (Proverbs 18:21) "For by your words you will be justified, and by your words you will be condemned." (Matthew 12:37)

The Gospel of John states that, "In the beginning was the Word...and all things were made through him." (John 1:1-3) We are told that the Word became the life of men and dwelt among (within) us. Whatever you speak, whatever you think (the silent word), when it is charged with constructive energy or destructive energy, will produce after its kind and become your expression of life. With SRT you can use the power of your word to delete any conscious or subconscious programs that are causing problems from your "bio-computer" and put in new, positive, constructive programs and it works!

Jesus was able to perform many miracles, because he knew that the physical world and everything in it is an illusion. He could change the illusion of illness into the illusion of health, the illusion of death into the illusion of life, the illusion of two fish and seven loaves of bread into the illusion of food enough to feed 5,000 men, women, and children. He could walk on water, because he recognized that the illusion of the physical body could walk on the illusion of the physical Sea of Galilee. Above all, Jesus knew that he was spirit created in the image and likeness of the one great Spirit called God, and that like God, he was unlimited. He stated time and again that what you believe and what judgments you make determine the course of your life.

There is, according to Spirit, only one thing that is not illusion—God. And no one really knows what God is. We only have beliefs about God, which are mostly erroneous and often counter-productive to a balanced, harmonious, and productive expression of Life.

CHAPTER 4

Chart 2. The Programs and When They Are Established

ॐ ॐ

Seven of the thirteen programs of Spiritual Response Therapy were originally defined by David B. Cheek, M.D., and Leslie M. LeCron, B.A., as aids in hypnotherapy—identification, imprint, experience/trauma, benefit, organ language, self-punishment, and conflict. Dr. Clark Cameron took those seven programs and began to work with them. As a result of his studies, he added past life programs. With this set of eight programs, Dr. Cameron developed a very powerful system that he named Response Therapy.

I trained with Dr. Cameron and after starting to work with the system, I found five more programs: past lives in other dimensions, future lives, inheritance, fear, and discarnates. I also learned to work with a spiritual committee that I call the High Self, so I named this system Spiritual Response Therapy.†

Sometimes a current life difficulty is caused by only one type of program, such as imprint. In which case, there may be one or more imprint programs involved. Other times, there may be several different types of programs involved, such as conflict, benefit and self-punishment. In this case, there may be one or more of each of the three types of programs.

All possible combinations are to be considered when searching for the problem areas in the subconscious mind that are affecting the client's life in some restrictive way. These areas are not mutually exclusive. There are times when it is extremely difficult to categorize the problem as being a specific program type. Although the subconscious mind does seem to differentiate by indicating several program types, when the programs are researched, they may be so linked that they cannot be isolated.

The items listed on the chart are defined below in order, left to right, with the inner half-circle discussed first.

Inheritance

Inheritance is usually a belief that you picked up in another life and carried over into the present life. I call it the luggage you packed and brought in with you. Inheritance programs are usually running (active) and causing subtle or even strong discordant, and often, obvious effects in the present life.

Another common source of inherited beliefs is your parents' genes. These beliefs can be eliminated by asking your High Self to clear them.

You can also inherit a belief from someone else by associating with them and accepting and believing what they say. Usually, this form of belief is not as common as the genetic belief.

Identification

Fortunate indeed is the person who was raised by parents who were good examples. The person who received love and affection, and

---

†After the first edition of *Your Mind Net* was published, I discovered "Master Programs" – courses of study we construct by planning lives which have specific spiritual challenges. Example: If we feel we have not yet learned enough about forgiveness or love, we may set up a life where we must face and overcome unforgiveness and hate. These programs require extra steps for clearing. A complete discussion of Master Programs and how to clear them was included in my second textbook on SRT, *"Soul Re-Creation."*

who had a happy childhood is most blessed. When the father and mother express love toward each other and toward their children, it establishes a positive identification with one or both of the parents in the mind of the child, and sets a good example for the child to follow. There is then a good chance that the child will also experience a loving, meaningful relationship when they reach adulthood and choose to marry. Whereas, attitudes of insecurity, unhappiness, or rejection by parents toward each other or toward the child during the child's early years may strongly influence the child in a discordant way.

Everyone is a copy-cat to some degree. Children begin to copy their parents at a very early age. We have all witnessed small children playing house or school and it is astounding and considered very amusing when a child expresses the characteristics and habits of an adult. The adult has become the role-model of the child and the child has already begun to practice the traits that will be his/her identification with the parent, teacher, adult, authority figure, etc. Often, the source of the harmful program is an identification with one or more adults or significant other from the client's childhood.

There is also dis-identification; a person may perceive some discordant trait in another and adamantly insist that they will never be like that. This will also result in discordant energy and cause problems between them.

Imprint

An imprint is a message that is received by the subconscious mind during a time of emotional stress. The imprint becomes fixed in the subconscious mind and then is carried out when outer circumstances are right for a triggering of the message. Because most imprints are totally erroneous or greatly exaggerated, they cause the person to act in specific, disruptive patterns until the imprints are released and replaced with a beneficial message. It is as though a posthypnotic suggestion was made and is being carried out without the conscious volition of the subject. The person simply has no control over it. Only by understanding the subconscious programs can they take control through clearing the old message and reprogramming.

Experience/Trauma

Experience is, of course, involved to some degree with all of the other programs. If you did not experience something in the outer, there would be no record in the subconscious mind, no sense of wrongdoing, and no reason for self-punishment, etc. All of life is experience in one form or another.

Traumatic experiences may create deep-seated phobias. Some of which are: fear of the dark, claustrophobia, fear of heights, fear of falling, and so forth. One man had an appetite for fish. However, he was always careful to pick all of the bones out before starting to eat. If he happened to miss a bone and bit down on it while chewing, he could not continue to eat the fish but would throw it away. Work with Spiritual Response Therapy revealed that he had choked to death on a fish bone in a previous life and the trauma was imprinted in his subconscious mind.

A single traumatic experience can have far reaching impact on many areas of a person's life. One female client had gone to a movie when she was seven years old with an older brother, age nine, and a younger brother, age five. A man with deep-seated emotional problems, a total stranger, molested her. As a result of this single experience, she held discordant energy on both of her brothers and on her parents, especially her father because he was not there to protect her! Later, it had a discordant effect on her relationship with her husband. As we worked to clear programs, the trauma of this experience repeatedly entered into some phase of the process.

Sexual molestation (invasion of privacy or assault upon the personal sanctity of being) establishes the highest discordant charge of all the programs. One woman had one hundred percent discordant energy and zero positive on a cousin. There was only one reason for the discordant energy and it was an experience/ trauma program. When asked if she knew what it was, she said, "I don't want to talk about it." I told her it was all right as I felt I knew what it was any way. She looked surprised and asked me what I thought it was. I told her it was sexual molestation. She was then able to talk about it and admitted that when she was four, her teenage cousin had masturbated in front of her. Although there was no physical contact, it was an invasion of her physical and emotional space by a sexual act and carried a heavy charge.

Benefit

Benefits, also called motivations, may be either positive and constructive or discordant and destructive. Example: For a person who does not receive the longed-for love, attention, and positive stroking necessary for their well-being as a child, a benefit program of justification may cause the person to act in such a way as to draw attention to themselves; even though the result of doing so may cause discomfort or even pain. Discordant energy can be held against a parent, sibling, spouse, child, or another person because they did not give the expected love and attention.

Another form of benefit is self-punishment. It can be a desire to punish yourself for not living up to what your parents expect you to be. Or, a person may become ill in order to receive the sought-for attention they desire. There is no limit to the physical or emotional disorders people can create for themselves in order to get their stroking. We are very inventive creatures and can create reasons of benefit for all kinds of perceived hurts with or without any valid or rational basis for doing so.

Conflict

Many of your reactive attitudes toward other people may have their roots in conflict. Although there seems to be a basic human drive to love and to be loved, we often will not allow ourselves to be loved or to be loving because of conflict. A simple definition of conflict is "a want" colliding with "a can't" or with a "they (the other person/s) are not worthy" or "I am not deserving." You may want to love a person but are kept from doing so because they are not loving toward you and therefore do not deserve your love. For instance, one of the common reasons for a person not experiencing prosperity is a belief that they are not worthy. So the desire to prosper is in conflict with the belief of unworthiness.

There are many sources of conflict. Soon after birth an infant begins to run into all kinds of taboos. Some of these taboos are helpful. Others are destructive and can cause conflict later on in life. These taboos can be verbalized as: "No! That is wrong." "You can't." "You mustn't." "You shouldn't." Conflict may be a source of strong guilt which can cause programs of self-punishment. If you have such programs, you may inflict mental, emotional, or even physical pain on yourself. Many people are completely unaware of the source of conflict in their life since they have repressed the awareness of the causes.

Self-Punishment

How wonderful it would be if we as human beings were free from the need and desire to punish ourselves. There has not been one person with whom I have worked who has not been, at least to some degree, caught up in self-punishment. The reasons are myriad, and the slightest perceived infraction in thought, feeling, or action can trigger an act of self-punishment.

There is often a "catch twenty-two" aspect to self-punishment in which you punish yourself by exhibiting the exact behavior you are punishing yourself for expressing. A child may have received repeated messages of worthlessness from one or both parents or even from an older sibling who has become a parent figure or role model and they will establish a program in the subconscious mind to punish themselves for being unworthy by acting in such a way as to be unworthy. Thus, the program perpetuates itself in a constant downward spiral.

Often the programs are deeply entrenched and require repeated work to uncover and release. One person with whom I worked had sixteen self-punishment programs. All of them were identified and cleared in one two-hour session. During the following week she did several things to cause herself pain. At her next session I asked if she were punishing herself and received a "no" response. I then asked if she were beating up on herself and received a "yes" response. There were fifteen reasons for her to beat up on herself. The reasons were identified and after clearing them the person's life began to change immediately. Sometimes it takes a lot of clearing work to rid a person's subconscious mind of self-punishment programs, but it is well worth the effort, for the increased health, happiness, and success they begin to experience.

The masochism (self-punishment) can be so deep-seated that suicide, extreme injury, terminal illness, or even death by accident results. Accidental death or terminal illness is simply another way (through a subconscious decision) of committing suicide and may be more acceptable to the person than using a deliberate, conscious means of leaving the body.

Many people have committed suicide in former lives and may have a subconscious suicide program trying to manifest itself in this life. These people may not have succeeded in driving the life out of the body or may not even have attempted to do so, but to a greater or lesser degree, they have succeeded in slaying their good. There seems to be a destructive tendency or self-limiting, self-punishing tendency in the way they are living their life. Nothing good seems to come to them and if it does, they will find some way to destroy it. Once the suicide program is uncovered and released, things always change for the better.

Organ Language

Organ language comes in two categories: body comparison and body statement. One person with whom I worked was holding discordant energy on his mother because of a body comparison. Questioning the subconscious revealed that he hated his nose which was like his mother's nose.

The other category, a statement about the body, can actually cause the body to create a psychosomatic disorder. A person may develop throat problems because of an often repeated statement that "I can't swallow that," referring to something that is going on in their life. An often repeated statement such as, "That gives me a headache," can and may result in headaches. Working with clients in Spiritual Response Therapy certainly makes one aware of the power of the words we speak.

Some of the common statements we hear every day are, on the surface, seemingly harmless yet there is a great possibility of the words manifesting in a very destructive way. Here are a few common statements that we would do well to drop from our language. "That just slays me." "That just burns me up." "That gives me a pain in the neck" (or some other place). There are a host of such statements. Some of them seem laughable but they are not. Look at this one: "That just tickles me to death." Sounds laughable, yet the subconscious mind does not know the meaning of a joke and simply pro-

duces what it is told. The subconscious is strictly subjective in nature and follows literally everything it is told.

The wise ancients knew about the power of the word. There are several statements in the Bible that describe this phenomenon. "Death and life are in the power of the tongue: and they that love it shall eat the fruit thereof." (Proverbs 18:21) "For by thy words thou shalt be justified, and by thy words thou shalt be condemned." (Matthew 12:37) "So shall my word be that goeth forth out of my mouth: it shall not return unto me void, but it shall accomplish that which I please, and it shall prosper in the thing whereto I sent it." (Isaiah 55:11) "Thou shalt decree a thing, and it shall be established unto thee..." (Job 22:28) The Gospel according to John states that in the beginning all things were created by the Word. Since you are made in the image and likeness of God, you also create conditions in your own life, body and affairs by your own spoken and unspoken word. I don't know about you, but I don't wish to be "tickled to death." I would much prefer being "tickled to life!"

Past Lives

Some of the people for whom I do clearing work believe in previous lives or reincarnation. Many others do not. Yet, seldom have I ever worked with a client for any length of time without encountering past lives as one of the reasons for some current problem. Not wishing to convince someone against their will that they have lived before, I completely research the first eight programs listed on Chart 2 in an attempt to find the reasons for the problem, before presenting the area of past lives. After exhausting the first eight program types, if there is still a reason for the problem, I simply hand the chart to the client and ask them to use the pendulum to find the program. They are quite surprised to see the pendulum swing toward "past lives." I always verify the movement by asking if it is a program of "past lives."

Past Lives—Other Dimensions

In the beginning of my work with Response Therapy, the program of "Past Lives—Other Dimensions" was not known to me and so was not shown on the chart. This program was discovered in rather a strange way. I was working with a person who had been cleared of every conceivable emotional and psychological reason for experiencing a rather severe case of rheumatoid arthritis. While the subconscious reported through the pendulum that there was no physical or psychological reason to continue to be debilitated with the arthritis, the condition was persisting with only slight relief. In the next session I handed the client the pendulum and asked:

Q. *Do you have arthritis?* (-)

Q. *Is there any reason for the arthritis?* (-)

Note: to save space I use (-) for a "no" response and (+) for a "yes" response.

Obviously, this was in error, and I was not willing to accept it as a final answer. Fortunately, I had recently been shown how to work with another level of consciousness which I refer to as my High Self. At this level of consciousness, there appears to be a link between my mind and the other person's mind.

Holding the pendulum myself and using the chart I asked my High Self if there was any reason for the arthritis that had not yet been found. The answer was "yes." When I asked how many programs there were, the pendulum moved in the direction of the number six on one of the charts. I verified this response by asking if there were six and only six programs. I received a "yes" response.

The next step was to find what kind of program was causing the arthritis. In this case, when I asked what the program was, the pendulum was moved back and forth across the bottom of the chart. This was rather confusing, so I again asked if there was any reason for the problem of arthritis. Again, there was a "yes" response.

I remembered that many years ago I had been told by an enlightened person that I had experienced lives on other planets. This was an intriguing and very interesting concept, but it certainly could not be proven at that point in time and space. Anyway, I took a chance.

Q. *Is this a program of past lives on other planets?* (+)

Q. *How many lives are there?* (six)

Q. *There are six past lives?* (+)

Q. *Any other programs?* (-)

That is how I learned that the subconscious mind differentiates between past lives on Earth and past lives in other dimensions. If both are involved in a problem area, the pendulum will be moved by the subconscious mind to indicate first one and then the other. Should the counselor be unaware of the possibility of past lives in other dimensions, problems caused by these lives will simply not be discovered for clearing.

Future Lives

As eternal spiritual beings, we are not bound by time and space. As pointed out by Albert Einstein, in the absolute or spiritual reality, time and space do not exist. This is the premise behind the late Jane Roberts' concept of simultaneous multiple lives as described in her many Seth writings. Any life—past, present, or future—may impact the current life.

When a subconscious program of interference from future lives came up during a case, I was, needless to say, surprised, intrigued, and unable to explain this except as an example of an alternate reality. If Spiritual Response Therapy had not proven to be logical, accurate, and helpful to people, I would have been happy to forget that future lives influenced this case. There are a lot of unanswered questions regarding the whole issue of future lives which only continued work and experience will resolve. However, since anything that is held in the subconscious mind as a discordant block can be released through this method, it is only necessary to clear the energy held on future lives (real or imagined), and move on.

Discarnates

There are several types of blocks that can interfere with the movements of the pendulum. One form is discarnates—people who have made their exit from the physical body but not from the physical earth space. There are many reasons why a discarnate does not leave the earth vibration and go into the realms of higher vibration. Dr. Edith Fiore's excellent book, *The Unquiet Dead*, explains this phenomena and its impact on over 70 percent of her patients.

Whatever the reason for the discarnates failing to go into the light, they can be a very real detriment to the person who becomes host to them. Many times, after the movements of the pendulum have been established and work is started on the actual clearing process, the system will breakdown—it simply stops working. Upon asking High Self, I find that the person has one or more blocks from some form of interference (on Chart 1). Refer to chapters 7, 8, and 21 for instructions on how to remove these blocks.

Not only do discarnates sometimes keep the system from working, but they may cause mental, emotional, or physical problems for the person who is the host. For example, one client had developed an overpowering addiction to chocolate. She just could not seem to leave it alone. It made no difference that she knew it was not good for her—she simply had no control. We found she had five discarnates and three of them were addicted to chocolate. She had picked up the discarnates two years before I worked with her while she was under anesthesia for an operation.

Many times the client has sufficient energy to override the conflicting energy of the discarnates and the system will work very well. When this happens, you may be completely unaware of the discarnates and they will continue to influence the client in subtle ways. No longer do I assume that if the system works, the client is free from discarnates. I begin each session with a check to see if the client has any blocks and if any are found, they are removed.

Fear

Fear programs are often encountered when researching a client's blocks to a balanced, productive life. They can have their inception in this life or anywhere back to the beginning when only the GODHEAD existed.

When Programs Are Established

Chart 2 lists in the outer half-circle several possibilities as to when programs can be established. Once you have identified the type of program causing a particular current life problem, the next step is to determine when the program was established.

Parallel Lives

Parallel lives can be compared to a clump of birch trees; there is one major root cluster, but several trunks. Another analogy is a tree with one trunk, but many branches. In some paranormal studies, parallel life is called "bi-location." Regardless of any attempt to describe parallel lives, it is difficult for most people to believe that they can be in more than one place at a time. The thing to remember is that you are created in the image and likeness of God (Genesis 1:26-27), and God is everywhere. You are a spiritual being/living soul, expressing through a physical body. Therefore it stands to reason, if you will simply open your mind to the idea, that the soul can express through more than one body at the same time.

There can be a few or many lives in a set of parallel lives. The minimum I have encountered is five and the greatest is 5,849. Some people are living more than one set of parallel lives, and each set has been in a different galaxy. The discordant energy experienced in a parallel life can bleed over into the current life and cause problems. Regardless of the number of lives in a set or the number of sets, enough lives must be researched until all lives in all sets can be cleared and blocked from interfering in the current life ever again. When High Self is asked to clear and block, it is as though they put up a wall between each parallel life and between the parallel lives and the present one.

Womb

The soul may decide while in the womb, and attached to the fetus, that it is going to encounter some discordant experience or challenge when it is born. For example, there may have been many lifetimes when the soul became discouraged or disillusioned with life and committed suicide. Therefore, the challenge may be to face the possibility of suicide and overcome it. When it is indicated that the womb is the point at which the soul set up a program, the discordant energy (challenge) may be found on Chart 4.

Past Life

A program can be established in a past life. The past life experienced could have been on this planet, another planet in our solar system, or even in another galaxy. The circumstances and experiences can be similar to or identical to lives on this planet. Each planet is a school room where the soul chooses lessons to be learned, and even on this planet, from country to country, the school rooms and lessons are similar.

Bardo

According to the Whitton and Fisher book, *Life Between Life* (page 10), "bardo" is a Tibetan term that means "space or time between lives" and High Self says the definition is correct. Prior to incarnating in the present body, you were in the Bardo. You met with a Light Council (your High Self), which consists of two or more beings of higher consciousness. You reviewed your akashic record and considered what you needed to work on in this present life. You chose the galaxy, planet, country, parents, style of body, and the lessons or challenges you needed to encounter, learn from, and work through. Sometimes a soul is reluctant to incarnate because the challenges they choose to face may be difficult and painful. You may come in kicking and screaming, but come in you do.

Programs said to be established in the Bardo have their roots in past or other lives. You must research and clear the root cause, so your next question will always be: "When was the root cause established?"

Birth

The soul may, at the point of birth, set up an energy they need to face and work through, or they may start a discordant pattern carried over from a past life. Usually all you have to do is locate the discordant energy on Chart 4 and clear it.

Present Life Already Happened

Let's suppose that, when you ask when a program was established, the pendulum is moved to indicate "Present Life Already Happened." Using a chart with numbers (either Chart 2 or Chart 3), ask for the age when the program was established. If the pendulum swings toward 10, then ask if it was established at the age of 10. If you receive a "no" response, ask if it was established at the age of one (in which case, the zero is being ignored).

At other times, you may ask when a program was established and the pendulum will swing between the zero and the ten. Since a time frame of ten years is too broad, ask that the zeros on the chart be ignored and the age given in single digits. Then, when the pendulum is moved between two numbers on the chart, say 30 and 40, you know the age is between three

and four. Since it is always wise to verify the answers received, you would then ask:

Q. Was the program established between three and four years of age?

Another possible response to the original question, "When was the program established?" could be that the pendulum will swing between two numbers on the chart which are higher than nine, such as between ten and twenty. Verify that the program was established between the ages of ten and twenty. Then, ask for the second digit. The zeros will be ignored. If the pendulum swings toward 30, then the second digit is three. Again, you would verify this answer by asking if the age the program was established was age thirteen.

Present Life Yet to Come

Remember that you laid the plans for this life in the bardo before you incarnated. You could even have planned the time and method of leaving the body. One client's child had done just exactly that. He had planned to leave the body at age five through an auto accident. That program was cleared and the child is seven years old and still in the body. These things cannot be proven, however, the many changes manifested in thousands of client's lives as a result of this work are proof enough for me. Therefore, I have to accept as fact that the person had pre-planned their death and that plan was changed.

Death and Transition

Both of these usually mean the same thing, a death experience in a past life. However, it could be a planned death in the future of this life or a major shift, or transition, in the status or condition of the person in this present life. One person registered a transition at age seven when they were ripped away from friends and family and an established way of life on the East Coast, and forced to move to California. This action registered as a form of death and a whole new structure of life.

Future Life

Future lives are alternate realities. I call them dream lives as they are set up to handle some unresolved past life energy or situation that needs to be experienced and finished. According to my High Self, they are lived in other dimensions of planets. If you are living future lives on this planet, they are in the 55th dimension. Once they have been researched as required by Spirit, they can be cleared and they are finished. They are no longer being lived and have become part of the past life total.

Past Lives—Other Dimensions

These are lived in other dimensions on other planets. High Self says every planet has life forms similar to Planet Earth. However, if we journeyed to another planet such as Mars or Venus, we would not see the life forms because they would be in another dimension of those planets. Past lives in other dimensions are researched the same as any other past life.

Parallel Universe

According to one quantum physicist I met, they believe that we live in every parallel universe at the same time. High Self says that is not accurate. We can have lives in only one parallel universe. They are researched and cleared the same as any other life and the scenarios and discordant energies are pretty much the same as we encounter on this planet.

CHAPTER 5

Chart 3. Cast Of Characters
ᔕᓁ ᓄᔔ

Whether researching the present life or another life—be it past life, future life, parallel life, past life in other dimensions, or parallel universe—determining the cast of characters is vital and important to an understanding of the problem area. Let's start on the inside left to explain this chart. Some of the items are pretty obvious, such as male and female, and need no explanation.

Androgynous

Androgynous simply means that the body form may be both male/female or neither male/female. I have never bothered trying to get more particulars regarding this form.

Guide, Guardian Angel and High Self

Every soul has three standing committees working with them. They are called guide, Guardian Angel, and High Self committees. Each committee may consist of from one to an infinite number of spiritual beings. The High Self is like the hub of the wheel and is the coordinator of the work that is done by SRT.

Guardian Angels have the responsibility of protecting the soul from pain. So it is important to make them aware that a person does not experience pain through Spiritual Response Therapy, otherwise, they may block the research effort. Ask frequently that all members of your committees and councils be cleared, educated, elevated, harmonized, balanced, and uplifted and that proper supervision be established.

Thought

When thought is indicated, it is usually discordant thoughts that the individual holds in their mind. Sometimes it is indicated when the soul is out of the body. The soul is reviewing the discordant energies from past lives that it has not yet cleared up and is planning a physical life in which they can do the needed work.

Cherub and Seraphs

Both Cherubs and Seraphs are angel forms and when they are indicated in a past life as part of the cast, they are usually serving in one of the three offices—guide, Guardian Angel, or High Self.

Separates

Separates are fairly high level spiritual beings. There are offices in the spiritual realms where they can work and be of service. They have no desire of working in the available offices, so they enter planetary vibrations and attach themselves to incarnated souls. Their energy interferes with the movements of the pendulum and can cause wrong answers. It is not necessary to clear their programs. There are places in the spiritual realms where they can be cleared. Just ask High Self to send them where they can be cleared. Warning: If you clear them, they will tell their friends and you'll have so much interference all you'll be doing is clearing separates, and you won't be able to clear yourself or any clients. Have them cleared and removed by the High Self and ask that a shield be put up to keep more separates from interfering.

Discarnates

Discarnates are souls who have left the physical body, but not the earth plane. Chapter 21 is devoted to a full discussion of discarnates.

When discarnates of any kind are indicated in a past life, they need to be cleared and removed. Just ask your High Self to do the work.

Dark Energy

Dark energy in a past life is usually anything on Chart 4 that one or more of the cast may be carrying. When dark energy comes up, ask if the person is incarnated, and whether they are male or female.

Family Group and Other Groups

Family groups need no explanation. Other groups may be an army, a religious group, or a political group. I may ask if someone else is involved and receive a positive response. Then, when I ask what they are, I may get a circular movement of the pendulum. That is the way my High Self tells me we are dealing with a group. I may then, if I wish to do so, use a number chart to determine the number of persons in the group.

Light Energy

Everything we see is simply a vibration of light that is stepped down until it becomes visible to human eyes. Light energy, when given as part of the cast in another life, is the package of energy that we call the Spiritual Body/living soul (light being) created in the image and likeness of God.

Father, Mother, Etc.

Father, mother, brother, etc. may designate family members. They may also designate a member of a religious movement. Father could be head monk, head priest, or high priest. Mother could be high priestess or mother superior. Brother could be monk or priest, and sister could be priestess or nun. Son could be a student monk or student priest, and daughter could be a student priestess or student nun, postulant or novice.

Grandparent, Etc.

Grandparent may simply mean an older person.

Angel

Angel, when it comes up, may be serving in one of the three offices—Guide, Guardian Angel, or High Self.

Light

Light is the energy that each soul was before we were created as a light being, in the image and likeness of God.

God

Usually, this is a soul serving on the High Self committee.

Uncle, Aunt, etc.

Uncle, aunt, husband and wife are self-explanatory. Other relationships will simply require more questioning. For instance, the cast may be sister and uncle. The sister may actually be a niece. High Self will tell you what the relationship is when you learn to listen and ask.

CHAPTER 6

Chart 4. Discordant Energy

One of the first things I discovered when working with SRT was that it is not what happens in a past life or at any time that causes the problem to persist or re-establish itself, it is the unresolved or carried-over energy attached to the situation. That is why the Bible reiterates time and time again that forgiveness is necessary if we would be free.

Technique

Chart 4 has an inner and outer circle. Notice that in the inner circle at the top of the chart on either side of the center line there are two words—Inside and Outside. These words are used to designate which circle the energy may be found in.

To determine what the energy is, you will first need to determine in which circle the energy is listed. Then you will need to know on which side of the circle the energy is listed. To do this, hold the pendulum over the hub of the wheel and ask where the energy will be found.

Q. *Is the energy on the inside or outside of the chart?*

Let's say that the pendulum is moved to point at the word, Outside. Always verify the responses.

Q. *Is the energy listed in the outside circle?*

If you receive a "no" response, you most likely are blocked. Clear all blocks and interference before doing further research. (Refer to Chapter 8.) Allowing confusing or inconsistent answers is one of the ways in which High Self alerts you to the fact that you have interference, perhaps from discarnates. Discarnates may block your efforts by sometimes giving correct answers and sometimes incorrect answers. If you unknowingly accept wrong answers, you end up with a scenario that is not correct and therefore the program cannot be cleared. That's why it is so important to verify your answers.

If you receive a "yes" response, ask:

Q. *Is it on the left or right side of the outside circle?*

Continuing our example, if the pendulum swings to the left of the center line, the next question would be:

Q. *Is the energy I need to find on the left half of the outside circle?"*

When an affirmative response is received, ask to be shown the word. Let's say that the pendulum is then moved to indicate "Hate of Women." Confirm the response by asking if the energy is "Hate of Women." A positive response would indicate that you read the movement of the pendulum correctly.

Then ask if there is another word that needs to be found. If a "yes" response is received, ask where the next word will be found. Continue this process until there is an indication that no other word needs to be found.

In other life research, usually, it is only necessary to find who the person was and what the energies were that they held. Then the program can be cleared.

CHAPTER 7

Technique—The Basic Steps of SRT
ॐ ☙

The heart of Spiritual Response Therapy is research and clearing. Working with Spirit (High Self), we research the cause of negative programs and belief systems. Then, we ask High Self to clear the program. Additionally, we may support this process of mind purification with affirmations and energies that align us with our divine selves.

As a spiritual being, you already possess the qualities you need to use SRT—connection to Spirit, and your own intuition. All you need is patience and practice.

Attuning Yourself to Spirit

All things have a starting point. Because SRT is a system based on working with Spirit—your High Self—the starting point for SRT is prayer. Your prayer does not have to be long or complicated. Rather, it can be quite simple, yet profoundly effective, such as the prayer Jesus used: "The Father and I are one." Do not pray with the hope of changing God, because the purpose of prayer is to attune yourself to God. The prayer my High Self taught me to use is: "The Father and I are one. We work together as a team."

> My Father is working still, and I am working...Do you not believe that I am in the Father and the Father is in me? The words that I say to you I do not speak on my own authority; but the Father who dwells in me does his works. (John 5:17, 14:10)

Affirm your oneness with Spirit and you will be guided to perform marvelous work for many of your brothers and sisters.

Making Certain You Are Clear

You cannot work accurately or effectively with SRT unless you are clear and working with your High Self. Some people unknowingly work with discarnates (souls who have left their bodies but not the earth plane) or with satanics, demonics, or dark forces (discarnates that have even stronger negative energy). Their work is inaccurate and misleading and it takes a long time to research and clear programs. In fact, you can never clear all programs when working with discarnates because you do not receive correct answers. So make certain you are a clear instrument and that you are working with your High Self. Here are the questions I ask before starting the actual research for myself or for a client.

Q. *Do I have any blocks or interference? (If you receive a "yes" response, use Chart 1 and the information presented in Chapters 7 and 8 to research the cause. Then ask High Self to clear the block or program. Continue to ask this question and clear blocks until you receive a "no" response.)*

Q. *Will I get correct answers? (If you receive a "no" response, you must work with Spirit and the charts to clear yourself. Continue to ask this question and clear blocks until you receive a "yes" response.)*

Q. *Will I receive wrong answers? (If you receive a "yes" response, you must work with Spirit and the charts to clear yourself. Continue to ask this question and clear blocks until you receive a "no" response.)*

Q. *Am I working with my High Self? (If you receive a "no" response, ask that you be cleared and that you be placed in direct contact with your High Self. Continue to ask this question until you receive a "yes" response. Use Chart 3 and ask who you are working with. Pendulum should be moved to indicate High Self.)*

Q. *Can I start work now? (If you receive a "no" response, you must again work with Spirit and the charts to clear yourself.)*

Sometimes you may be so blocked that you cannot even use the pendulum. In that case, speak the releasing statements included in Chapter 8. Or, you can work with another person who knows SRT to clear your blocks. As you clear more and more of your blocks and programs, you should find it easier to get clear answers.

Keeping Yourself Clear

Do not talk about what programs have been found and released as there is a chance of recharging the energies. If you find it difficult not to talk about the situation, and many people do, speak of it in the past tense and always end on a positive note. Affirm something like: "I found that I had held all of that discordant energy on...because...but now I know that it is all released and I feel very light and free."

Also, you should make a conscious effort to clear your own programs daily. Because you are on this planet to learn and grow, you will often encounter new programs and negative energies. Some programs may not be activated until you reach a certain age, or until some event or circumstance triggers them.

When you work with other people to help them clear their discordant programs, you not only bless them, you bless yourself. High Self assures me that your own energy clears in the process.

The Worksheet

The main goal of working with a client is to clear all of their basic programs. To make certain that the client is as clear as possible and that I don't miss anything, I use a worksheet. It includes a list of the significant relationships and the areas of life that are commonly affected by programs. There is a copy of this worksheet in Appendix B. I suggest

that you complete a copy of this worksheet before you begin clearing your programs or anyone else's. This worksheet can be a significant aid when interviewing clients in regard to the problem areas in their lives.

There is room at the bottom of the second page for noting additional issues of concern. These areas may include such things as overweight, addictions to alcohol, drugs or food, fear of success, claustrophobia, agoraphobia or fear of heights. Or, the client may be concerned because they cannot seem to prosper or because they continually destroy relationships with the opposite sex. Checks can be made to see if there are any subconscious blocks to healing or if there are some psychosomatic reasons for a particular illness. The possibilities are variable and endless. Everyone has his or her problem areas that may be cleared and although there are similarities from person to person, there are also definite differences. Every person is unique and wonderful in their complexity and diversity and each person must be treated individually through Spiritual Response Therapy.

Percent of Positive and Negative Energy

On the worksheet, there are spaces where you can record the amount of positive energy and the amount of negative energy held on each item. When the clearing is complete, the percent of positive energy should be one hundred percent and the percent of negative energy should be zero.

You determine the percent of energy by using a chart with numbers on it (Chart 2 or 3) and asking:

Q. *What is my percent of positive energy on...?*

The pendulum will be moved to indicate one of the numbers. Verify that this information is correct by asking:

Q. *Is my percent of positive energy on...45 percent?*

When you have established the percent of positive energy, you ask questions in the same way to get the percent of negative energy. Do not add the two percentages together to see if they add up to 100%. They are not related in that way. Indeed, each of them could be 100%. Or, they could be any other combination.

Recording Your Research

Because the charts can reveal a lot of detail, you will probably want to record your research on a sheet of paper as you work. As you ask each question, make note of the response. This is not only a valuable record that you can give to your client at the end of a counseling session, it is also a very effective way to track your progress as you work, so that you do not miss any steps.

What You Will Need to Clear Programs

Once you have attuned yourself to Spirit through prayer and cleared your own blocks, you are ready to research and clear programs.

To research and clear programs you will need:

- A pendulum
- The charts in Appendix A
- A completed worksheet
- Paper on which to record your research

You may also want to have a copy of Figure 7-1 so that you can easily refer to it and make sure you do all the steps and in the correct order. This figure can also be found in Appendix C where it is printed on a page all by itself.

Two Methods

There are two general methods of proceeding with the system. The usual, or basic, method is the one used when you are doing a complete clearing for a client. The other, less common, method is used when a client asks about a specific area of their life that is causing them difficulty or pain. Both methods use the same basic steps. The second method requires that you ask a couple extra questions regarding the number of programs involved in the situation before asking the basic research questions.

The Basic Method

If you are doing a complete clearing for yourself or a client, you simply begin by asking: "Is there a program to research?" If you receive a "yes" response, you ask each question in succession as listed in Figure 7-1. Each of these questions is explained in detail later in this chapter. After you have acquired enough information to clear that program, ask: "Is

there another program to research." Continue in this way until you receive a verified "no" response to this question.

The Second Method

On occasions when a client asks about a specific area of their life, you use the same procedure as for the basic method but you restrict your questions to the topic the client has asked about. In this case, you first determine how many programs are blocking the client in the specified life area, then you determine how many programs need to be researched.

Usually, you do not need to research all the programs because we so often repeat life scenarios lifetime after lifetime in what I call "carbon copy" lives. Generally, it is necessary to clear only one or two of these carbon copy lives.

Determining the number of programs

Let's assume that your client's financial condition has been chaotic, and they just cannot seem to get ahead. Debts are piling up, and they fear they may be out of a job soon, so they choose to start clearing the reasons why they are blocked in their prosperity. Ask the following four questions:

Q. *Does [client's name] have any blocks to prosperity?*

Q. *Does [client's name] have any blocks to receiving his/her good?*

Q. *Is [client's name] in the flow of good?*

Q. *Is [client's name] open to receive.*

If you receive a positive answer to either of the first two questions or negative answers to either of the third and fourth questions, there is something that needs to be cleared.

The next step is to ask how many reasons there are for the blocks to the client's prosperity.

Q. *How many reasons are there why [client's name] does not believe he/she has the right to prosper?"*

The pendulum will swing toward (point at) a number on the chart.

After you have gotten an indication of the number of reasons for a particular program, verify it. Let's say that the subconscious mind has caused the pendulum to point at the number 60 on Chart 2. Ignore the zero and ask:

Q. Are there six programs blocking their prosperity?

If you receive a "no" response, ask if the number is sixty or more. You may also have interference or the exact number may not be on the chart. To clarify, ask questions which can be answered "yes" or "no", such as:

Q. Is the number of programs a two-digit number?

Another way to determine numbers, is to assign values to the upper left and right corners and to the top center of the chart. If the pendulum is moved to indicate the left corner of the chart, I know the number is in tens; if the pendulum is moved to indicate the middle of the chart, the number is in hundreds, and if to the right corner, the figure is in thousands or greater.

Whichever way you use, verify the response, then ask:

Q. What is the first digit?

Q. What is the second digit?

Again, verify the response. For instance, if the first digit was the number one and the second digit was the number six, this would make the number sixteen. So you would ask:

Q. Are there sixteen programs blocking their prosperity?

There are times when the number of reasons goes up and up beyond all possibility of handling the situation. Or the pendulum may move across the bottom of the chart indicating that the number of reasons is infinite. Should this happen, simply ask what the first program is, research, and clear it. Then ask what the next program is, research and clear it, etc., until there are no programs remaining. I often find that clearing one program clears many other programs without further research.

If the responses aren't making sense, then you probably have interference. Ask:

Q. Do we have interference?

If you receive a "yes" answer, you must clear it before proceeding. Refer to Chapter 8.

Having established the number of programs that are blocking the client's prosperity, you now need to know how many programs need to be researched.

Q. How many of these programs need to be researched?

Determine the correct number in the same way that you determined the number of total programs. Be sure to verify the answer.

From here on, the procedure is exactly the same as in the basic method. Begin with the second question listed in Section B of Figure 7-1: "What is the program?"

The SRT Procedure

A. Clearing to Work

Do I have any blocks or interference?

Do I have any program or energy blocks?

Am I working with my High Self?
    Using Chart 3: Ask, "Please show me who I am working with."

Will I get correct answers?

Can I start work now?

B. Steps in Research (90% of all research is past life research.)

1. Is there a program to research?

2. What is the program? (Use Chart 2.)

3. When was it established? (Use Chart 2.)

4. Find the cast of characters (only major participants). Use Chart 3. List across the page. For past life research, find out who the client was, and then, who the remaining cast members were. For present life research, just find out who the other cast members are.

Example:	Client	Other	Other	Other	Other
	Female	Husband	Son	Daughter	Etc.

5. Was there hurt or harm?

6. Who was harmed? By whom?

7. Was it mental, emotional or physical harm?

8. Was it simple, serious or death?
    (Mental or emotional harm can be early death or suicide.)

9. If there wasn't any harm, ask whose energy needs to be cleared. Then use Chart 4 to find the energies.

10. Ask "Is this enough information to clear the program."
    If the program cannot be cleared, you may need to research one or more of the following items:
    • Someone else's discordant energy
    • One, or more, additional lives
    • Find the ages of the cast
    • Find who one or more of the cast is in this life

    When researching parallel lives, ask: "Is this enough information to clear the program? ... the life? ... the set of parallel lives?" You may need to research more lives to clear the program and/or the set of parallel lives.

11. Ask High Self to please clear all lives. (When researching parallel lives, be sure to ask High Self to clear and block all parallel lives between each other and between the parallel lives and this life, so that they can't bleed through.)

Figure 7-1. The Basic SRT Procedure

Six Basic Steps for Researching and Clearing Programs

Once you have attuned yourself to Spirit through prayer, cleared your own blocks, and obtained permission to work, you are ready to research and clear programs.

Step 1. Identify the First Program that Needs to Be Researched and Cleared

Use Chart 2 to determine if there is a program that needs to be researched. (In this book, I use the symbol "+" to represent a "yes" response, and the symbol "-" to represent a "no" response.)

Q.   Is there a program to be researched for [client's name]? (+)

Q.   What is the program?

The pendulum should swing to indicate one of the programs in the inner arc of the fan on Chart 2. For information about the items listed on this chart, refer to Chapter 4.

If "Discarnates" is indicated, you know that the client has discarnates or some other block or interference listed on Chart 1. Ask High Self to clear the client and put up a shield for the client and for you. Repeat the question. If the pendulum again points to "Discarnates," use Chart 1 to determine exactly what is blocking. Refer to Chapter 8 for instructions on how to clear the block or interference. When the client is completely clear and you have verified this, return to Chart 2 and repeat the first question: "Is there a program to research for [client's name]?"

On your notepad, write the answer you receive (i.e. inheritance, imprint, etc.). For a complete explanation of the program refer to the chapter of the same title.

Step 2. Determine When the Program Was Established

Again use Chart 2, but this time the answer will be in the outer arc of the fan.

Q.   When was the program established?

More often than not, Spirit indicates that the program was established in past lives.

Step 3. Find the Cast of Characters

If the program was established in a life other than the current one (past life, past life in other dimensions, parallel life, parallel universe, or future life), you need to determine who you were in that life. When doing research for a client, you determine who they were in the life. Always, and I cannot stress this enough, find who you or your client were first, then find the rest of the cast members. Ask:

Q.   Who was I in this other life?

The pendulum swings to indicate the role played by you.

Or ask, "Who was the client in this other life?" The pendulum swings to indicate the role played by the client.

Now you need to find who else was involved in the event that caused the program to be established. Occasionally, there may be no one else involved. However, usually there are several major players. You do not need to research minor participants in the scenario.

Q.   Is there someone else involved who we need to find? (If yes, ask "Who?")

Continue to ask this question until you have identified all the major players.

Sometimes the subconscious wants to give you a list of people (often the family members) as the cast. When this happens, I ask the subconscious if we can lump the family together as a group, if we do not need to know who particular individuals are. Here is how High Self indicates a group to me.

Q.   Is there someone else involved? (+)

Q.   What were they? (The pendulum moves in a circle.)†

Q.   Is it a group? (+)

If I receive a "yes" response, I ask what the basic unit size of the group is. If the pendulum is moved to indicate the left corner of the chart, I know the number is in tens; if the

---

† The direction in which the pendulum swings, clockwise or counterclockwise, has no meaning in and of itself. In SRT, there are only two meanings to a circular motion of the pendulum. These meanings depend on the question asked. Either it is a working circle or a group is being indicated instead of a single individual. Do NOT carry over into SRT any other interpretations of clockwise or counterclockwise which you may have learned in other systems. They do not apply.

pendulum is moved to indicate the middle of the chart, the number is in hundreds, and if to the right corner, the figure is in thousands or greater. When the basic unit is a single digit, High Self moves the pendulum directly to the number.

Q. *What is the basic unit? (The pendulum is moved toward the upper-left corner, indicating the figure is in tens.)*

Q. *What is the first digit? (7 is indicated by pointing to 70; ignore the zero.)*

Q. *What is the second digit? (3)*

Q. *So the total is 73? (+)*

Q. *What are they? (Sister)*

So, this is a group of sisters. Since the number is so large, it is probably a group of religious sisters (nuns). The roles of sister, brother, father, and mother can indicate either biological relationships or religious figures. Just ask your High Self which it is.

If the pendulum had moved in a circle in response to the last question instead of pointing at "sister," it would mean they were a mixed group of people.

Step 4. Identify the Negative Energies

Often, the last piece of information you need in order for the program to be cleared, is the negative energy you (or your client) carried away with you. This is important because the retention of this negative energy can be a chief cause of disease and disharmony in this life and future lives. First, you must find out if you sustained harm.

Q. *Was there hurt or harm? (If yes, ask the next question.)*

Q. *Who was harmed? (The pendulum swings to indicate which person was harmed.)*

Q. *Who caused the harm? (The pendulum swings to indicate which person caused the harm.)*

Sometimes you may get the indication that the person harmed him or herself, which could mean suicide.

Q. *Was the harm mental, emotional or physical?*

If the pendulum is moved to indicate the left corner of the chart, I know the harm was

mental; if the pendulum is moved to indicate the middle of the chart, the harm was emotional, and if to the right corner, the harm was physical.

Mental or emotional harm can be early death or suicide. If physical is indicated, ask the next question.

Q. *Was it simple harm, serious harm or death?*

If the pendulum is moved to indicate the left corner of the chart, I know the harm was simple; if the pendulum is moved to indicate the middle of the chart, the harm was serious, and if to the right corner, the harm was death. When the pendulum is moved in a circle, it means that all three forms of harm were involved

If there wasn't any harm, ask whose energy needs to be cleared. Then use Chart 4 to find the energies. Refer to Chapter 6 for instructions in how to work with this chart.

Q. *What was the energy? (The pendulum swings to indicate the first energy.)*

Q. *Is it [state the energy you thought was indicated]?*

Q. *Are there any other negative energies? (If you receive a "yes" response, ask what the energy is.)*

Continue to ask this last question until you receive a "no" response. Again, remember to verify all responses. Record all your answers on your notepad.

It is at this stage that your intuition may come into play. Now that you know the players, the level of harm, and the energies, you can often get a general picture of the situation or event. This situation will often bear some resemblance to a difficulty or problem in the current life.

Step 5. Clear the Program and Associated Negative Energy

There are two ways to clear programs and the associated negative energy. One way is to state aloud releasing statements, as explained in Chapter 3. The second, and easiest way to clear a program is to ask Spirit, your High Self, to do the work. Just ask these questions:

Q. *Is this enough information to clear the program." (+)*

If the program cannot be cleared, you may need to research one or more of the following items:

- Someone else's discordant energy.
- One, or more, additional lives.
- Find the ages of the cast.
- Find who one or more of the cast is in this life.

Continue research until the entire program can be cleared. When researching parallel lives, ask the following series of questions: "Is this enough information to clear the program?... the life?... the set of parallel lives?" You may need to research more lives to clear the program and/or the set of parallel lives.)

Q. *Can you clear this program for us? (+)*

Q. *Will you clear this program now? (+)*

Q. *Please clear and replace with good.*

The pendulum will be moved in a circle to indicate Spirit is working. Once the old programs have been cleared and the new program is put in, the pendulum is moved in a forward and back "yes" motion to indicate that the work is complete. (When researching parallel lives, be sure to ask High Self to clear and block all parallel lives between each other and between the parallel lives and this life, so that they can't bleed through.) Always check to make certain the work is complete.

Q. *Are the discordant beliefs removed? (+)*

Q. *Has a new, positive program been installed? (+)*

Say "Thank you."

On occasion, a "no" answer is received when the subconscious is asked if the problem is cleared. Should this happen, check each area to see if something else has come up from the subconscious. Simply use the pendulum and ask, "Is there some other program we have not found yet?" I cleared one person of nine past lives where suicide was involved. When a check was made to see if he was clear, he was not. Further questioning revealed that there were nine more past lives where he had committed suicide. He simply was not ready to handle

eighteen past-life suicides at one time so his subconscious mind only revealed half of them to clear first.

Step 6. Repeat the Research for the Next Program

When Spirit has finished clearing the first program, find the next program to be researched and cleared, beginning the process all over again.

Q. *Is there another discordant program that needs to be researched and cleared? (+)*

You may repeat this process many times before all the programs have been cleared.

Learning to Work with Your High Self

Learning to work with your High Self makes the system more powerful and allows a more in-depth purification. Your subconscious mind does not know all of the possibilities and areas of how and where programs are established. The High Self has more information. Also, the High Self can clear programs without using the releasing statements.

You may wish to determine who you are working with by using Chart 3, Cast of Characters. Hold the pendulum over the point where the lines intersect on the chart, ask that all blocks and interference be cleared until you are working with your High Self. The pendulum should be moved in a circle (I call it a working circle),† either clockwise or counterclockwise, and finally point to the High Self. That is the indication that you are working with the High Self and are ready to start researching. Once the research is completed, and you are given a positive response when you ask if the program can be cleared, just ask them to clear and replace with positive energy. They will, again, go into a working circle and when the work is done, you will receive a "yes" movement indicating that the work is finished.

Logical Process to Follow

There is a logical process to follow when using Spiritual Response Therapy that can save a lot of back-tracking and extra work. Suppose there are four reasons for a problem: programs of

---

†The direction in which the pendulum swings, clockwise or counterclockwise, has no meaning in and of itself. In SRT, there are only two meanings to a circular motion of the pendulum. These meanings depend on the question asked. Either it is a working circle or a group is being indicated instead of a single individual. Do NOT carry over into SRT any other interpretations of clockwise or counterclockwise which you may have learned in other systems. They do not apply.

trauma, benefit, identification, and imprint. In the order given, the first program (trauma) would have the highest discordant charge and the last one given (imprint) would have the smallest discordant charge. Regardless of which program is given first, you always start with identification if it is listed as one of the programs. Next, research the imprint program, if it is given as one of the reasons. After that investigate the trauma program. Only then would you research the benefit program. This order can save a lot of work simply because the benefit usually has its roots in the identification, imprint, and trauma programs. (See Chapter 13 for an explanation of why this is so.)

When You Are Lost or Stuck in Research

I receive many calls for help from students and practitioners of SRT. They tell me that in their efforts to research some programs, they are blocked or lost and do not know what to do. The first thing I do is make certain I am clear and working with my High Self and that I will receive correct answers. Then I ask the following questions.

Q. Are they having a problem getting correct responses? (If I receive a "yes" response, I ask the next question.)

Q. Is there a clue on one of the charts as to why? (Again, if I receive a "yes" response, I ask the next question.)

Q. Which chart? (Use a chart with numbers on it. The pendulum will point to a number from 1 to 4.)

Often the block will be on Chart 1— Blocks and Interference. If this is the case, use the standard procedure for clearing blocks and interference as explained in Chapter 8. After all the blocks have been identified, I ask High Self to clear them. Then, I check to see if there are any other blocks, research them and ask High Self to clear them. When I cannot find any more blocks, I ask the next question.

Q. Are they lost in procedure?

If this is the problem, I review with them the basic steps previously discussed in this chapter.

CHAPTER 8

Removing Blocks and Interference
ℰ ℭ

There are many potential blocks to working with SRT and many forms of interference which cause incorrect or confusing responses. This chapter focuses on how to remove any block or interference. Blocking energies can be either beings or programs, whereas interference comes from individuals. Blocking energies can be found on any of the four charts. Sources of interference are found on Charts 1 and 3.

You may experience blocks from the following sources:

- Discarnates, imprints, or other negative energies (Chart 1)
- Energy from other lives, discarnates, or self-punishment programs (Chart 2)
- Guides, Guardian Angels, High Self, other spiritual helpers and counsel, or other beings listed on Chart 3
- Discordant energies (Chart 4)

You may experience interference from the following sources:

- Discarnates, or other beings listed on Chart 1
- Discarnates (Chart 2)
- Beings listed on Chart 3

Removing Unknown Blocking Energies

High Self may indicate that the blocks are not listed on any chart. My High Self indicates this by giving a "no" response across the bottom of Chart 1. In this case, just ask if the block can be cleared without research.

Chart 1, Blocks And Interference

This chart lists many common blocking energies, beings and programs. High Self can remove all of them.

Discarnates

Discarnates are souls who have left the physical body through what we term death, but have not left the earth vibrations. They have ninety hours in which to leave the planet and enter the spiritual realms. If they do not leave within that time, they become earthbound and cannot leave Earth and enter the spiritual realms without help.

When a person is under hypnosis and a past life is being researched, it is as though there is no time or space and the life is being lived at the moment. The scene is very real and all of the pain and emotions experienced during the past life may be felt while under hypnosis. While researching past lives with SRT, the pain and emotions are seldom experienced. However, if discarnates were present in the past life, in parallel lives, or in past lives in other dimensions, they can come into the present life and block movements of the pendulum. They need to be cleared and removed.

The many types of discarnates (in aura, in possession, in past lives, satanics, demonics, dark energies, dark forces, satanic forces, and demonic forces) are described in-depth in Chapter 21. Briefly, satanics are discarnates who are carrying bad energy such as hate, ego, sexual promiscuity, fatigue and so forth. Demonics have worse energy: hate of women, hate of God, spiritual suicide, despair, greed and others. Dark energies are any energies from Chart 4. Dark forces is a group of discarnates with dark energies. Satanic forces is a group of discarnates with satanic energy. Demonic forces is a group of discarnates with demonic energy.

Separates

Separates are fairly high level spiritual beings. There are offices in the spiritual realms where they can work and be of service. However, they have no desire of working in the available offices, so they enter planetary vibrations and attach themselves to incarnated souls. Their energy interferes with the movements of the pendulum and can cause wrong answers. It is not necessary to clear their programs. There are places in the spiritual realms where they can be cleared. Just ask High Self to send them where they can be cleared. Warning: If you clear them, they will tell their friends and you'll have so much interference all you'll be doing is clearing separates, and you won't be able to clear yourself or any clients. Have them cleared and removed by the High Self and ask that a shield be put up to keep more separates from interfering.

Imprint of Brain Damage

A common subconscious message that may interfere with effective use of the pendulum is an imprint of brain damage. Fortunately, once the brain damage imprint is found, it is easy to remove from the subconscious computer. Ask High Self to clear the imprint or repeat some releasing statements† such as the following:

> *I release my belief, perception and judg-*
> *ment that the doctor (nurse, parent, or*
> *other) said I have brain damage. I release*
> *all need or desire to believe that I have*
> *brain damage. I release all need or desire*
> *to believe anything but that my brain is*
> *perfect and functions with one hundred*
> *percent accuracy. I am wise and intelligent.*
> *I learn quickly and easily and I have a*
> *marvelous ability to retain and to instantly*
> *recall all that I have seen, read and experi-*
> *enced.*

Once the releasing statements are made and the subconscious mind has been given the new statements, check to make certain you have accomplished your purpose.

Q. *Do I have a message of brain damage? (-)*

Q. *Do I have any brain damage? (-)*

Q. *Is my brain one hundred percent perfect? (+)*

Q. *Do I learn quickly and easily? (+)*

Q. *Do I have the ability to retain and to in-stantly recall all that I have seen, read and experienced? (+)*

If there is an indication that the clearing work has not been fully completed, ask again to be cleared or simply repeat some more releasing statements.

Imprint—Other

Imprint—Other involves past lives. There are several things that register in the soul records as imprint of brain damage from past lives. They are: Alzheimer's, Downs Syndrome, syphilis, or statements of insanity.

Discordant Thought Forms

Charles Fillmore, co-founder of Unity, a religious movement, proposed that every thought produces a form which becomes part of the collective race consciousness. This form can be maintained for a long or short period of time depending on the amount of energy attached to it. It is these discordant thought forms that a person attracts or creates that can block correct responses. The discordant energy given to these forms can and often does conflict with a person's life. Some people who are sensitive can even feel the energy.

Some people are blocked by the discordant thought forms they are constantly sending forth into the ethers around themselves. These thought forms, when there is enough energy involved, may cause the pendulum to move in erratic and nonsensical ways. When you find that thought forms are blocking release counseling, ask High Self to clear them or use releasing statements.

> *I release my belief, perception and judg-*
> *ment that there are any thought forms*
> *blocking the use of this system of counsel-*
> *ing. I release all need and desire to have*
> *any thought forms block me from using this*
> *system. I release all need and desire to*
> *believe that there are any discordant*
> *thought forms blocking me now. I release*

---

†Since High Self can clear all programs, releasing statements are not necessary, but they can be of great benefit in certain situations, as explained in Chapter 3.

all need and desire to believe anything but that all discordant thought forms are now dissolved and that this system works perfectly.

If there are still thought forms blocking, go through the releasing statements again. Continue to make releasing statements until all systems are clear and the process of Spiritual Response Therapy works.

Thought forms always have an energy, either positive or discordant, attached to them. The more energy you devote to a thought form, the longer lasting the thought form may be. For a while at least, the thought form has an existence. Recently, while working with a client, we found a very persistent thought form. This discordant form had been invested with so much energy by the client that it was beginning to think for itself. It believed that if it could gain enough discordant energy from the client, it would establish an identity of its own and become an individual expression separate and apart from its creator. This may sound far fetched and ridiculous, but it has influence in our lives.

God created us from the fabric of Himself by projecting his thought into a form. Although most people believe they have an existence separate and apart from their Creator, it is impossible. If you were separated from God, you would no longer exist. It is the same with a thought form that you create, it has no existence except as an extension of your own mind and energy. When you dissolve the energy held on it, it ceases to be. It could never exist by itself even if it could find a way of separating itself from the person who created it.

Conscious Control

Some people have a fear of losing control so they set up very strong programs of conscious control. You may have established such a program of self-control for your life. When work is started with the system, your fear of losing control through the use of a pendulum may kick in and your subconscious mind may block pendulum movements. Also, fear of finding out your inner programs can block movement. Use releasing statements to release the fear of losing control or of finding out what the subconscious programs are. I have yet to find one person who will not respond to patient, persistent work to clear their blocks and resistance. Here are some releasing statements to use:

> *I release all fear of answering the question. I release all resistance to answering the question. I release all fear of working with the subconscious mind. I give the subconscious mind permission to answer the question.*

Other

Sometimes you will encounter a block that is not on Chart 1. The pendulum will be moved to indicate "other." Just ask your High Self if they can clear, remove and block whatever is causing the problem. If you get a "no" response, ask if there is a reason. You may need to research the reason or High Self may need to clear the reason before it can clear the block.

Blocks to Working With SRT

There may be times when the pendulum responses will not be clear and definite, or, inconsistent information will be given when you are clearing a program. Or sometimes, the system just quits working. If this happens, make some releasing statements to release all resistance and fear of working with the system, then try again. If it still does not work, there may be one or more blocks or interference. The first thing I do is check with my High Self to see if there are any blocks or interference. (See Chapter 7 Learning to Work with Your High Self.)

Q. *Does the client have any blocks or is there any interference to using the system? (+)*

Q. *Are they on Chart 1? (+) (Use the chart and pendulum to determine what the blocks are.)*

You may have one or more of the blocking energies on Chart 1. Clearing all areas, so productive work can proceed, may take some time. However, asking the High Self to clear the blocks is usually quick and easy. Great patience is required when you release one group of discarnates and find that another group has been picked up. When more are picked up, ask for a shield to keep them out. Or, simply ask that all blocks and interference be cleared and the necessary shields put up. Fortunately, once you release discarnates from past lives in other dimensions, you cannot pick up others from that source.

It has often been said that you are what you eat. It is more true that you are what you think and feel. Most people do not care what they think or what emotions they attach to their thoughts because they do not realize that what they think and feel becomes their subconscious programs. Nor, do they understand that what they hold in the subconscious mind becomes the outer expression of their lives—good or bad.

Spiritual Response Therapy helps rid the subconscious mind of discordant thoughts and the associated energy that keeps the thought form alive. It can also be used to program the subconscious mind with new positive thoughts and energy. It is up to the individual to continue the program of releasing, becoming aware daily of discordant thoughts and emotions, and releasing them immediately before they take root in the subconscious mind. Never is there a time when humans are completely free from discordant energies and thoughts. Maintaining an existence free from discordant thoughts and emotions requires purpose, direction and constant work.

Asking Unclear or Double Questions

Sometimes what may be perceived as a block or a confusing answer, is simply the result of asking an unclear question or a double question. "Are you five foot four or six foot two?" is a double question. If one of the heights is correct, the answer may be a "yes—no" movement, a circle, a forty-five degree swing, or there may be no movement at all. If neither height is correct, the answer would be "no."

There are times when changing the wording in a sentence only slightly will change the answer. In the beginning you may wish to write out the question before you ask it. Then you have a record of what you have asked so you do not repeat questions. Also, the written questions are a guide when the releasing statements are made. If you have the slightest suspicion that you are receiving a wrong answer, reword the question.

Removing Blocks on Chart 2

Several items listed on Chart 2 may be a source of blocking energy. They are past lives, past lives in other dimensions, self-punishment programs (which usually have their roots in past lives and past lives in other dimensions), and discarnates.

About twenty-five percent of the people with whom I have worked have had some blocking energy based on past lives or past lives in other dimensions. Many of these people were able to overcome the blocks without research, while others could not use the pendulum until the blocks were cleared.

Self-punishment programs are also common causes of blocks to using a pendulum, and are usually based in past lives or past lives in other dimensions. Some people also punish themselves for coming into this life and often block themselves in every aspect of living, not just in using a pendulum. Clear self-punishment programs in the usual manner, as explained in Chapter 7.

Removing Blocks on Chart 3

Included on Chart 3 are beings who are part of your spiritual councils (advisors). When High Self indicates that the blocking energy is on Chart 3, ask which ones are blocking. Then ask what Spirit recommends be done with them. High Self provides us with three options:

- Clear them.
- Clear and remove them.
- Clear, remove and replace them.

For example, here are the questions you would ask:

Q. *What is the blocking energy on Chart 3? (Guides)*

Q. *Do you want to take them out? (-)*

Q. *Do you want to clear and remove them? (+)*

Q. *Do you want to clear, remove and replace them? (+)*

If High Self does not want to remove the being who is blocking you or your client, ask High Self to clear the being. If High Self wants to remove and replace the being(s), ask that they be replaced with higher level beings.

To make questioning easier, I made the following agreement with my High Self. When I ask the question, "What do you want to do with them?" High Self moves the pendulum to the upper-left corner of the chart to indicate clearing the energy. To indicate clearing and removing them, High Self swings the pendulum to the center of the chart. To indicate clearing, removing and replacing them with others, High Self swings the pendulum to the upper-right corner of the chart. After receiving an answer from your High Self, simply ask them to do what they have indicated. If you set up an agreement or contract with your High Self similar to mine, it will simplify the questioning process. See Appendix G for other agreements you can make with your High Self which will further simplify the process.

Case study: Subconscious cover up

The subconscious mind may try to cover up a program because of an imprint. Amanda's subconscious mind tried to cover up. We had cleared one area of relationship and decided to work on clearing the discordant energy she held on her mother. Amanda spent some time talking about her mother and the picture she painted was not a good one. She had a lot of energy on her mother as her conversation about her mother was very discordant. We tried to work with the subconscious by using the pendulum and ran into trouble.

Q. *What is the discordant energy on your mother? (There was no movement of the pendulum.)*

Q. *Is there any discordant energy on your mother? (-)*

Q. *Is there any reason to hold discordant energy on your mother? (-)*

Obviously, this was not true. Releasing statements† were used again and again to clear subconscious resistance and nothing worked. Finally, I began to work with my High Self.

Q. *Are there any blocks or interference to using the system? (+)*

Q. *How many forms are there? (one)*

Q. *What is the form? (discarnates)*

Q. *How many are there? (one)*

We had previously cleared this client of discarnates.

Q. *Is the discarnate someone the client knows? (+)*

Q. *Is it her mother? (+)*

Permission was received to clear the mother and High Self did so. After clearing, a check was made to make certain she had gone into the light and had not just stepped aside. The system still would not work. I had the client make some more releasing statements and tried again. No go! Back to High Self.

Q. *Is there a block in the subconscious mind? (+)*

Q. *Does it have anything to do with the biblical injunction to honor your father and mother? (+)*

Q. *Does that mean she cannot hold discordant energy on her mother? (+)*

Q. *Any other reason? (+)*

Q. *What is the area? (imprint)*

The imprint program turned out to be an often-repeated statement given to Amanda by her mother—"Shut up!" A lot of releasing statements were spoken by the client and we still could not get the cooperation of Amanda's subconscious mind. We had spent almost an hour trying to break down the resistance of the subconscious mind with no results. The imprint of "Shut up!" was just too strong. It is certain that in time the blocks to working with the subconscious mind and the pendulum could have been cleared. However, Amanda was anxious to get on with the process so I asked permission of my High Self to hold the pendulum and do the work. Permission was given and the programs were found and released.

Next, work was started to find the reasons for the discordant energy on her father—we ran into the same resistance. Knowing what the problem was, made it simple to get the subconscious mind to release the resistance and cooperate.

There always seems to be a way to overcome every block that the conscious or subconscious mind can devise. Sometimes it takes patience to find the answers. I find that working with the High Self is invaluable.

---

†Since High Self can clear all programs, releasing statements are not necessary, but they can be of great benefit in certain situations, as explained in Chapter 3.

CHAPTER 9

Inheritance

ℰ ℭ

An inheritance program is a belief someone else had which you took for your own. You may have inherited it from another life (past, parallel or future) or through a parent's genes or you may have adopted it from a close associate in this life. Most inheritance programs have their roots in other lives. Yet, they are usually "running" (i.e. active) in the current life and causing subtle or even strong discordant and often obvious effects. Regardless of the source of a program or how long you may have had it or how much discomfort it may have caused, High Self can clear all programs.

Usually, an inheritance program is a belief you acquired in another life and carried over into the present life. I call it the luggage you packed and brought in with you. You can also inherit a belief from someone else by associating with them and accepting and believing what they say.

Beliefs Inherited from Parents' Genes

Another common source of inherited beliefs is your parents' genes. Beliefs inherited from your parents come through their egg and sperm. Every cell is a minicomputer that stores a complete record of everything you have experienced through the five senses from the moment your soul attached to your body. Thus every cell in the body is a hologram containing the whole. (For an expanded understanding of this concept, you may wish to read some information on holography. I recommend the book *Stalking The Wild Pendulum* by Itshak Bentov.)

The soul can attach to the body at the instant of conception (the joining of the egg and sperm), anytime in the womb, or up to 2½ days after birth. Before the soul enters the body, the only programs that are registered in the cellular memory are those of the parents. This is because a parent's programs are carried in the cellular memory of the mother's egg and the father's sperm when they join to form the physical body of the fetus. This is often referred to in scientific terms as the inherited DNA in the genes.

Once the soul attaches to the fetus or newborn, it starts to pick up and register new information based on the beliefs, perceptions, and judgments presented to it by other physical beings. Remember, the soul is never even one day old—it is eternal. While attached to the fetus, the soul is aware of all that is being thought, felt, and acted out by those around it. After birth the child begins to dream as many as eight hours out of each day. Spirit says the soul is programming his or her soul (akashic) record into its cellular memory. This may take from a few hours to nine weeks, depending on the number of past lives, the age of the soul, and the amount of accumulated discordant programs. After the soul has completed the recording process, you can ask that the parents' and grandparents' programs (ancestral genetic beliefs) be removed from the cellular memory. That would mean that the body now carries in its genes, or DNA, only its own programming, which can be researched and cleared.

Inherited Belief in Disease

Spirit says that under no circumstances do you ever inherit disease. You may inherit the belief in disease because of genetic programming. Then, if you have a disease program of your own, or if you wish to use your parents' beliefs to punish yourself by experiencing their illness, you may. There is a limit on the number of generations of beliefs that we may inherit from our progenitors. The Bible says the third and fourth generation.

> *The Lord is slow to anger, and abounding in steadfast love, forgiving iniquity and transgression, but will by no means clear the guilty, visiting the iniquity of the fathers upon the children unto the third and fourth generation. (Numbers 14:18)*

"The Lord," in this case, means the law of mind expression. What we hold in mind and attach an energy to we create. Iniquity, or sin, is an erroneous belief or wrong thinking and feeling which causes a separation from good or God. This belief was set up prior to our first incarnation when we partook of "the tree of knowledge of good and evil" and incarnated. We often continue these beliefs lifetime after lifetime. Doctors help us to maintain error beliefs by insisting that we inherit disease from our parents. They also help us to attach a strong energy of fear to those beliefs that can then create the very disease that we fear. Job 3:25 states, "For the thing that I fear comes upon me, and what I dread befalls me."

Although the Scriptures state that genetic beliefs can go back three or four generations, I often find people who have carried them over eight and more generations, because they are constantly reinforced, generation after generation. If each generation would clear the inherited beliefs in disease and discord, those programs would not be passed on at all, as the chain would be broken. Also, it is important to not adopt and believe the doctors' or other people's belief that disease is inherited.

Technique

To research inheritance programs:

1. Ask when the program was established.
2. Find the cast of characters.
3. Determine the circumstances or get the discordant energy.
4. Ask High Self if the life can be cleared.
5. Ask High Self if the program can be cleared. (Research as many lives as necessary in order to clear the entire program.)
6. Ask for the exact number of lives involved in the program.
7. Find the energy/energies running in the current life.
8. Ask High Self to clear the program for all lives.
9. Once the program is cleared, return to the questioning process:

Q. *Is there another program to research and clear?*

Case study #1: Inheritance from past lives

Q. *When was it established? (past lives, Chart 2)*

Q. *What was Mary? (husband, Chart 2)*

Q. *Was anyone else involved? (-)*

Q. *What were the energies? (hate of men/self/ life/women, hate, and suicide, Chart 4)*

Q. *Is that enough information to clear the life? (+)*

Q. *Can you clear the program? (-)*

Q. *What was Mary in the next life? (husband)*

Q. *Was anyone else involved? (-)*

Q. *What were her energies? (hate of self, hate, and suicide)*

Q. *Is that enough information to clear the life? (+)*

Q. *Can you clear the program? (+)*

Q. *How many lives were involved? (2,784, Chart 2)*

Q. *Is the exact number of lives 2,784? (-)*

Q. *Is the exact number of lives 2,784, 1/2? (+)*

Q. *Does the 1/2 mean that some of the same energy is running and causing problems in this life? (+)*

Q. *What energy is running in this life? (hate of self)*

CHAPTER 10

Identification

&) C&

An identification program is a belief that you share a particular trait with someone you know. You may see a parent as thoughtless or self-centered, an uncle may be perceived as a stupid drunk, a romantic partner as deceitful, or an aunt may be seen as the black sheep of the family. You may even identify with yourself in a past life. When you identify with someone, you see yourself as being the same as they are (i.e. thoughtless, self-centered, etc.). Such beliefs result in discordant energy held on yourself and on the other person. Furthermore, there is often a connection between identification programs and self-punishment. In other words, you punish yourself for being like the other person. This results in even greater discordant energy. (Refer to Chapter 15 for an in-depth explanation of self-punishment programs.)

If you hold discordant energy on anyone, it is important to dissolve it. Discordant energy becomes heavy, limiting, and tiring and may set up destructive currents within the mind and body. These currents may block your expression of a greater good. They may also cause illness or other mental, emotional, or physical problems. Often, the problems that you are experiencing in your life have their roots in identification with a parent or another person you perceive as a role model.

Parents as Role Models

One or both of your parents become your role model as you grow up and you may take on many of their characteristics. This may be beneficial or not depending on whether the traits are positive or discordant.

"Honor thy father and thy mother, as the Lord thy God hath commanded thee; that thy days may be prolonged, and that it may go well with thee, in the land which the Lord thy God giveth thee." (Deuteronomy 5:16).

Many people believe honoring their parents means accepting everything they say and do without question. A better way to honor your father and mother is to live your life richly and fully to the best of your ability, not patterning your life after them, but expressing your own unique self. To do this effectively, let go of the beliefs about your parents that restrict you in any way.

Ernest F. Pecci, M.D., in his book *I Love You/I Hate You* states,

> We tend to take upon ourselves the characteristics of those people with whom we feel an emotional attachment. If we love someone, we tend to take on their moods and personality traits as a way of feeling their closeness when they are gone. Thus the child adopts its mother's moods in order to maintain a sense of her presence.

A person may take on certain traits of someone with whom they identify in an attempt to prove that they love that person, even if those traits are discordant and hurtful. There seems to be a basic drive within the make-up of the individual to love and to be loved. If the child does not get the nurturing and love they desire from a parent, they may copy the actions and characteristics of that parent in an attempt to say to the parent, "See, I am just like you. Please love me." (In the examples later in this chapter, Netta's case demonstrates this cry for love.)

Or, a person may act in such a way as to fulfill the negative beliefs held about them by those from whom they desire attention or love. Unfortunately, even discordant strokes are considered by many people to be better than none at all.

Dis-Identification

Sometimes people will exhibit "dis-identification." ("I will never be like that!") This binds the other person to you even though you might rather be free of the relationship. Regardless of whether the program is dis-identification or identification, it results in discordant energy which must be cleared.

Re-parenting Self

You have been given the faculties of wisdom and good judgment. It is not always wise to accept everything you receive from your parents or from another role model at face value. It may be good and right for them but may be very detrimental to your own expression of life. You must learn to make your own evaluations and determinations especially when you are a mature individual and are able to use your own reasoning abilities. "When I was a child, I spake as a child, I thought as a child: but when I became a man, I put away childish things." (1 Corinthians 13:11)

Many people, even after clearing all of the discordant energy on a parent, still do not have a good feeling about them. They may feel that the parent simply has not shown love or affection toward them over the years. I have my clients repeat the following.

I release my belief, perception, and judgment that my father/mother did not hold me, hug me, and love me every day until I was five. I release my belief, perception, and judgment that my father/mother did not hold me, hug me, and love me every day until I was ten. I release my belief, perception, and judgment that my father/mother did not hold me, hug me, and love me every day until I was fifteen. I release my belief, perception, and judgment that my father/mother did not hold me, hug me and tell me how much they loved me every day until I was twenty. I release my belief, perception, and judgment that my father/mother has not held me, hugged me, and told me how much they admire and appre-

ciate me every day of my life. I release my belief, perception, and judgment that my father/mother is not with me now any time I need them to hold me, hug me, and tell me how great and wonderful I am and how much they love me.

Use these statements for each parent individually, as desired. This seems to release the last vestiges of hurt and pain that the client has on their parents, and is a powerful way of mentally re-parenting self with positive messages.

Frequently after clearing the discordant energy on a parent, my clients will say something like Sam did:

"I have never had a close relationship with my father. He has always seemed distant and cold. Even if it was a special time such as Christmas or my birthday, his greeting would be unemotional and distant. Since you cleared me on my father, things have changed. The other day was my birthday. My father came over, walked up to me and gave me a big hug and his congratulations and best wishes. It was really a surprise. I cannot remember my father ever holding or hugging me when I was a child."

Protective Device in the Subconscious Mind

Occasionally it takes more than one session to uncover all the programs in the subconscious mind causing discordant energy to be held on a particular person. There seems to be a protective device (or layers) in the subconscious mind that prohibits too much material being revealed at one time. "Sufficient unto the day is the evil thereof" (Matthew 6:34).

Programs Dissolve Automatically

Many times when I have been working with a client over several sessions, and have succeeded in pinpointing and releasing discordant subconscious programs, there comes a time when most or all of the remaining programs simply dissolve. There is a definite shift in consciousness. Also, there are times when the moment the discordant energy that a client holds is revealed and the adjectives listed, the discordant energy is automatically dissolved. There is no further work to do on that particular person. They are clear. It is as if the conscious mind sees the unreasonableness or destructiveness of the programs and it is eager to change. This desire to change is communicated to the subconscious mind and the subconscious mind dissolves the remaining discordant energy.

Letting Go of False Gods

How wonderful it will be when humans stop worshipping "false gods" by identifying with others whether good or bad. For that is exactly what you do when you look to others as your pattern of life and not to God as your one and only Father/Mother image. When you "bow down to them and serve them," by accepting the discordant traits others reveal and the discordant consciousness they express, they become part of your own makeup and cause you to be like them. When you take upon yourself the discordant traits of others, you have set up the programs within your own subconscious mind that will cause you pain.

Whatever you set up in the subconscious mind, whether good or bad, will be fulfilled. It really makes a lot of sense if you look at the unconscious mind as the lord of your being. "I the Lord thy God am a jealous God, visiting the iniquity of the fathers upon the children unto the third and fourth generation" (Exodus 20:5). Spiritual Response Therapy is a marvelous and extremely powerful way of looking at the false gods you have accepted and which are causing you pain, and smashing them to bits.

Technique

To clear all discordant energy from your life, you can begin by releasing the discordant energy you have accumulated on your parents, or any other important person. Use a chart with numbers to determine both the positive and discordant energy you hold on people. Working with your High Self and SRT, you can get the positive energy to one hundred percent and the discordant energy to zero percent on everyone and everything in your life.

There is a worksheet in Appendix B that you can use to record the amounts of positive and negative energy held on a specific person, God and on life. This worksheet can be of great assistance in staying focused and organized as you do a clearing and it can help you do the clearing work in an efficient manner. All the

students in our Basic SRT course use this worksheet as they are learning and clearing themselves and others.

To research identification programs:

1. List adjectives that describe the person with whom you identify. If adjectives do not readily come to mind, Chart 4 may help you think of appropriate discordant energies.

2. Ask your subconscious mind if the person is actually like that. Often you will consciously see the person one way and subconsciously see them another way.

3. Ask if you think of yourself in the same terms.

4. Get the percent of negative energy on each trait.

5. Ask when this identification program was established. If past lives is indicated, you may need to research the past life/lives before this program can be cleared. (See case study #4 for an example of this situation.)

6. Ask if there is any other point of identification you need to find to make certain nothing has been missed. If the response is affirmative, you must search for other adjectives and complete all these steps for them.

7. Ask High Self to clear:
    a) the identification programs
    b) the resultant self-punishment programs
    c) the discordant energy you hold on yourself
    d) the past lives involved (if any)

8. Do a final check to make certain that there are no further discordant associations. Ask: Is there any program of identification to hold discordant energy on _____? (Ask this for both the other person and for yourself.)

9. If you receive a positive response, begin again with Step 1. Remember, the object is to get the discordant energy to zero percent and the positive to one hundred percent.

10. Once the program is cleared, return to the questioning process:

    Q. Is there another program to research and clear?

Case study #1: Cry for love

Netta loved her father deeply and had a positive energy charge on him of one hundred percent. She also had discordant energy of sixty percent. Her subconscious belief was that her father loved her but neither liked nor approved of her. Being a very sensitive person, it upset her greatly when her father called her a stupid jackass and told her she would never learn. The way she lived her life, it was almost as if she was trying to prove her father right so he would love her. She often did things to hurt herself mentally, emotionally, or physically, not deliberately or consciously, but seemingly without her desire or volition. Netta knew that chocolate and sugar upset her system and brought on migraine headaches. Yet, from time to time she would have a chocolate fudge sundae. It was simply her way, at least to some degree, of identifying with her father and seeking recognition from him even if that recognition of her was as a jackass. This pattern also showed up in her relationships with other important people in her life. Unfortunately for Netta, even discordant strokes were better than none at all. We began researching her inheritance programs by asking:

Q. *Netta, is your father thoughtless?* *(+)*

Q. *Are you thoughtless?* *(+)*

We continued this series of questioning until we had created the table of adjectives shown here:

Discordant Energy	Father	Netta
thoughtless	+	+
selfish	+	+
belligerent	+	+
self-centered	+	+
low-self-esteem	+	+
dreamer	+	+
starter/not finisher	+	+
pie in the sky	+	+
unrealistic	+	+
argumentative	+	+
hateful	+	+
vindictive	+	-
thoughtful	+	+
loving	+	+

Netta's father was her role model. The only discordant trait she was not copying was vindictive. Notice also that she saw her father as both thoughtful and thoughtless. She exhibited these traits in her own life at different times, sometimes against her will.

Additionally, our further research showed that Netta held discordant energy on all of the restrictive traits except argumentative and hateful.

Netta was typical of other clients. The identification with her father's discordant traits created self-punishment programs.

Releasing statements† were made to clear all of the points of identification that Netta had with her father—except, of course, that he was thoughtful and loving. For example, "I release my beliefs, perceptions, and judgments, and my needs and desires to believe that my father is thoughtless." You do not have to treat each discordant energy separately, but can simply add all of them to the first releasing statement. For example, you could say, "I release all belief, perception and judgment that my father is thoughtless, selfish, belligerent, and self-centered."

If you use releasing statements to clear a program, always use positive statements to replace it. After Netta made the releasing statements to clear the old programs, a new program was fed into the subconscious mind in the form of an affirmation: "I now completely accept and believe and instruct my subconscious mind to completely accept and believe on every level of my being that my father is loving, kind, thoughtful, considerate and always has my highest and best interest at heart."

When the old program has been released from the subconscious mind, the subconscious is open and receptive to anything you wish to put in. Remember that the new program may have a profound effect on your life and should therefore be carefully constructed in positive terms—so make it good!

The second and very important step is to release the discordant beliefs the client holds on themselves as a result of the identification.

---

†Since High Self can clear all programs, releasing statements are not necessary, but they can be of great benefit in certain situations, as explained in Chapter 3.

Netta was asked to repeat the following releasing statements. "I release all my beliefs, perceptions and judgments that I am thoughtless. I release all my needs and desires to believe I am thoughtless. I now completely accept and believe and instruct my subconscious mind to completely accept and believe on every level of my being that I am kind, thoughtful, loving, wise, orderly, constructive, peaceful, joyful, happy, and I always express my life in a positive way."

Next, I had Netta hold the pendulum while I asked:

Q. *Is your father thoughtless? (-)*

Q. *Are you thoughtless? (-)*

Q. *Are you holding any discordant energy on your father because of thoughtlessness? (-)*

At the end of the first session, the pendulum indicated that all of the programs causing discordant energy on Netta's father were cleared, e.g., there was one hundred percent positive energy and zero discordant energy on her father when she left that day.

During Netta's second session, we checked to see if she was still clear on her father, but found that she had more discordant energy on him than before. Netta revealed that she had called her mother immediately after her first session and rehearsed all of the reasons we had found for the discordant energy on her father and thereby reprogrammed her subconscious computer!

Do not talk about what was found and released as there is a chance of recharging the energies. If you find it difficult not to talk about the situation, and many people do, speak of it in the past tense and always end on a positive note. Affirm something like: "I found that I had held all of that discordant energy on my father because he was...but now I know that it is all released and I feel very light and free."

Case study #2: Dis-identification Discordant energy on life

Jim had seventy percent positive and eighty percent discordant energy on a woman he was dating in an on-again, off-again relationship. There were six reasons for the discordant energy he held on Jan and one of them was identification. Here are the results of the questioning:

Discordant Energy	Her	Jim
angry	+	-
resentful	+	-
deceitful	+	-
selfish	+	-
self-centered	+	-
low-self-esteem	+	-
liar	+	-

Each one of these was a point of dis-identification. Jim had none of these traits but resented that Jan did and so held discordant energy on her. Of course, the discordant energy was not hurting her. It was simply causing a lot of inner turmoil within Jim and binding Jan to him and him to her. He had been going with Jan for several years and simply could not understand why he stayed. As we progressed through the system, programs of self punishment and past lives were clearly the other reasons for the discordant energy Jim had on Jan. (See Chapters 15 and 17).

One of the areas I always clear with a client is the discordant energy they hold on life as they are experiencing it. Jim had sixty percent positive energy and sixty percent discordant energy on life due to programs of identification and past life.

Q. *Are you identifying with a relative? (-)*

Q *Are you identifying with Jan? (+)*

Q. *Does this identification have its beginning in this life? (-)*

Q. *Does this identification have its roots in a past life? (+)*

This particular identification went to the past life with Jan and the unhappy conditions experienced then. His association with Jan in this life was bringing up that old energy so that it might be dissolved now.

Case study #3: Discordant attitudes

The previous examples of identification were ones where discordant energy was held on a person. Let's take a look at a basic life problem created by discordant attitudes. Ella wanted to know why she sabotaged her communications with others. Questioning, using Charts 2 and 3, revealed that there was a reason of identification and it was with an aunt. Ella suggested that it might be her Aunt June. Using the pendulum and asking if it was her Aunt June, elicited a positive response.

The discordant energies we identified were: aggressive, self-centered, overbearing, insecure, and demanding.

All of these areas were cleared. Later on, when we were working on the energy that Ella held on herself, we found that there was again a reason of identification. This time she was identifying with her mother, her father, her grandmother and her Aunt June. We had previously done considerable work releasing energy she held on her parents, part of which was due to identification programs (see case study #6 below). Preferring to not repeat work already finished, I asked some questions.

Q. *We have already released the points of identification with the parents. Is there any more releasing necessary on them? (-)*

Q. *Are there other points of identification on the aunt? (+)*

The other points of identification with Aunt June were: selfish, self-centered, aggressive, independent (she was not supposed to be independent) and black sheep.

Note that some of the adjectives (self-centered and aggressive) reappear on this list. This does not always happen but it may when you are working on another person. You can clear your discordant energy of low self-esteem in regard to one person and it will show up again when you are clearing discordant energy on another person. Just clear it again—it is simply another facet of the jewel that needs polishing.

Q. *Do we need to make a list on the grand-mother? (+)*

The points of identification with the grand-mother were: stubborn, independent, man-pleaser, and a consciousness of lack.

Time and again, Ella had been told by authority figures in her life that she was just like her aunt and her grandmother. Now she was sim-ply trying to live out someone else's picture of her as being like her aunt or grandmother. Far too often we simulate the discordant traits of others rather than the positive ones. In this case, the discordant traits were copied because, when Ella did anything wrong, the comparison

was made with the discordant traits of the aunt and grandmother.

Case study #4:   Identification connected to a past life

Elijah wanted to know why every thing he sought to do to expand his spiritual awareness came to naught.

Q. *Are there any blocks to expanding your spiritual awareness? (+)*

Q. *How many programs are there? (eight, Chart 2)*

Q. *What is one of the programs? (identifica-tion, Chart 2)*

Q. *When was this identification program established? (birth, Chart 2)*

Q. *Are you identifying with the doctor? (+) (Logic would indicate that this must be a past life identification.)*

Q. *Is this an energy of identification from a past life with this doctor? (+)*

Q. *How many past lives are involved? (eleven)*

Q. *How many do we have to look at in order to clear this energy? (eight)*

Please note that the subconscious mind indi-cated there were eight reasons for the blocks and that eleven past lives were involved. How-ever, only eight of the eleven past lives needed to be investigated.

Many times there are a lot of past lives in-volved, and it is time consuming to look at every one of them. Usually, there are some carbon copy lives with only slight variations, and it is fruitless and time consuming to find out the infinite details involved again and again. The subconscious mind does not usually require that you look at all of them. One of Elijah's eight lives exemplify how identification and past lives are connected.

Q. *What were you? (husband, Chart 3)*

Q. *What was the doctor? (wife, Chart 3)*

Q. *Was there someone else involved? (pendu-lum moved in a circle indicating a group)*

Q. *Were there a lot of people involved? (+)*

Q. *Were you spiritually aware, a psychic? (+)*

Q. *Did your wife betray you? (+)*

(Being psychic was seldom considered as being spiritual, but, rather as being a witch.)

Q. *Did the people kill you?* *(+)*

Q. *Are you fearful that if you develop your spiritual awareness (psychic ability) again, you will be killed.* *(+)*

Elijah was killed in five of the previous lives. Also, he caused great pain and brought harm and death to others as a result of his misuse of spiritual powers (psychic abilities). The doctor was directly involved in five of these lives (all of the lives in which Elijah was killed) and was the triggering factor in this life to create the necessary conditions of mind to bring this whole situation into conscious awareness so that the energies involved could be released.

Due to the knowledge gained researching these lives and from asking questions of the subconscious mind, Elijah can release all of those old energies of past lives. He will be able to develop his spiritual awareness and use it in a wise and loving way as a blessing to himself and to others. He is a beautiful and compassionate soul in this life and his only desire is to be of help to others.

Case study #5: Identification with an uncle

A program of identification with a person may be a very simple one and quick to locate. Marian had a fairly high percentage of discordant energy on an uncle with only one reason, a program of identification. According to Marion, the uncle was a "stupid drunk."

Q. *Is your uncle a stupid drunk?* *(+)*

Q. *Is there anything else we need to find?* *(-)*

Q. *Is there any other reason for the discordant energy?* *(-)*

The necessary releasing statements† were said and then a check was made to see what the energy levels were. The positive energy was one hundred percent and the discordant was zero. No other action was required on the uncle.

Case study #6: Identification and self-punishment

While some identification programs are easily found and released, others may be very deep seated and extremely difficult to release. Ella was dealing with a lot of suppressed anger. She was also experiencing conflicting energy because of her deep seated desires to punish herself.

Q. *Do you have a lot of anger?* *(+)*

Q. *How many programs are causing the anger?* *(four, Chart 2)*

Q. *What is the first program?* *(identification)*

Q. *Who are you identifying with?* *(father)*

Q. *With anyone else?* *(pendulum moves to indicate mother)*

Q. *With anyone else?* *(male, we determined it was her psychologist)*

Q. *With anyone else?* *(female, a woman who was living in her home)*

Q. *Anyone else?* *(-)*

Identification with her father:

Q. *Is your father an angry person?* *(+)*

Q. *Do you see your father as perfect?* *(+)* *(Consciously, she saw him as a bully and a tyrant and had an intense hatred for him).*

Q. *Must you express anger to be perfect?* *(+)*

Q. *Is it wrong to be angry?* *(+)*

Q. *Is your anger destructive and harmful to others?* *(+)*

Q. *Is it destructive and harmful if you let it out?* *(+)*

Q. *Are you afraid you will kill someone?* *(+)*

Q. *Must you be angry to receive the attention you need?* *(+)*

Q. *Anything else on your father?* *(-)*

Identification with her mother:

Q. *Was she always angry but stuffed it?* *(+)*

Q. *Is anger all right if no one sees it?* *(+)*

Q. *Anything else on your mother?* *(-)*

Identification with her psychologist:

Q. *Does your doctor have suppressed anger?* *(+)*

Q. *Like your mother?* *(+)*

Q. *Anything else we need to know on him?* *(-)*

Identification with "K":

Q. *Is she an angry person?* *(+)*

---

†Since High Self can clear all programs, releasing statements are not necessary, but they can be of great benefit in certain situations, as explained in Chapter 3.

Q. *Does she remind you of your father?* (+)

Q. *Do you have to stay and take her anger?* (+)

Q. *Would you be wrong to run away from her anger?* (+)

As you can see, Ella was in a catch-twenty-two situation. On one hand, she must express anger to be perfect and on the other, she is wrong if she does express anger. Any discordant identification can damage a person's ability to live life freely and fully. However, a program like Ella's creates a double bind of "wrong if you do show anger and wrong if you don't show anger." Ella's programs were so deeply seated and reinforced, especially during her formative years, that even with Spiritual Response Therapy, it will take a long time to build a new solid foundation to replace the old one that was built on sand. Because of her deep seated anger and self-hate, she has caused irreparable damage to her body as well. It will take constant awareness of what is going on in her mind and consistent effort to build a new freedom of consciousness and, thus, a better life style.

CHAPTER 11

Imprint
ဆ က

Imprints are messages, statements or inferred ideas implanted in the subconscious mind during an emotionally charged time of life. They may be irrational, but because they are frequently established at an early age, often before a child is verbal or has conscious memory, they are simply accepted by the subconscious. Although imprints may be established in this or other lives and at any age, once an individual exercises judgment, the conscious mind discriminates between rational and irrational ideas and irrational ideas are no longer accepted into the subconscious mind. Adults do not commonly add new imprints, but they may have many imprinted messages from childhood and or other lives.

Imprints may be self-imposed or established by significant others or authority figures—parents, other relatives, doctors, or teachers, etc. They have a profound effect on emotions and behavior, influencing every aspect of life for years while the bearer may remain totally unaware of their presence.

When imprints are discordant, they have a very powerful potential of causing pain and trauma in a person's life. These subconscious messages, usually established at an early age, simply create all kinds of problems later when the circumstances are right for a triggering of the message. They cause the person to act in specific, disruptive patterns without conscious volition. The person simply has no control over their behavior.

When you look at these from a mature adult perspective, most of them are illogical, totally erroneous, or greatly exaggerated. Had the person been aware of their potential for destructive energy, they would not have accepted them in the first place. Once there is an awareness of these discordant programs, they can be released. Then, their discordant control is eliminated and a new program of growth and freedom is established.

Imprints of Brain Damage

Many of the people with whom I have worked have had imprints (messages/programs) of brain damage. They all confirm that they have had to struggle all of their lives to accomplish even the simplest things. The problems they experienced were not due to low IQ, but were caused solely by the imprint of brain damage. Once the brain damage imprints were removed, and a message of perfect brain functioning was put in, the person's life changed and usually in such a dramatic way that relatives and friends noticed the difference. In every case, when the imprint was removed, there was a dramatic change in the person's confidence, direction, and ability to express life in a more intelligent and fulfilling way. Had there actually been brain damage, nothing would have changed. Every client would still be acting out their life in a brain damaged pattern.

In only one of my cases has the subconscious mind reported that there was actually brain damage. The actual damage was about two percent. It was not affecting the person's ability to learn or to demonstrate their life in a positive way.

Most messages of brain damage are accepted at birth. This is especially true when the birth is difficult. Either instruments are used and the doctor makes some offhand remark about possible brain damage or some other factor is present leading some person in an authority role to make a statement of possible brain damage. Birth is a time of high energy and trauma and the subconscious mind of the newborn is totally open and receptive to what is being said and thought. It is usually believed that a child has no consciousness until after birth and they start to breath on their own, but this is simply not true. Imprints can even be made while the baby is still in the womb.

About ten percent of the people I have worked with have had messages of brain damage. This imprint often causes our research process to fall apart. We can usually establish the four directions for movement of the pendulum and even ask some check questions, but, when we start working to clear the client's subconscious mind of restrictive programs, logical answers are simply not forthcoming. The unspoken message from the subconscious mind seems to be: "How can I give logical answers, when my brain is damaged? Can a damaged brain be expected to function perfectly?" The answer, of course, is, "NO!"

Self-Responsibility

There is never a point in anyone's life when effort is not necessary to get on with getting on. Clearing discordant programs from the subconscious merely removes some of the major blocks to going forward. Whether a person proceeds to demonstrate their life in a full and productive way is still determined by their desire and energy to take the outer steps necessary to attain that full and productive life. Whereas one person may leap forward in great strides, the next person may accomplish very little in the way of change and a few may accomplish practically nothing. Some people seem to have developed such a high degree of inertia that it is difficult for them to break old patterns and to establish new ones. Doors can be opened to greater possibilities of expression, but each individual is responsible for moving through the door and going forward. New habits of thought and action need to be learned and persistently practiced to remain free and be successful.

Technique

To research imprint programs, use the standard technique explained in Chapter 7. There are two things that can help pinpoint the

energy on an imprint program. First, find out when the imprint was made. Next, find out who gave the message. (There may be more than one person. So be sure to ask: "Is there anyone else?") Then, ask questions in the usual manner in order to determine what the imprint is.

Case study #1: Imprints from parents and self

Tony had forty percent positive and thirty percent discordant energy on his mother. His subconscious revealed that there was only one reason for the discordant energy—an identification program. Tony talked about his mother so I could get a basic feeling for possible avenues for investigation and then we started the process.

Q. *Is your mother a discordant person? (+)*

Q. *Do you identify with that? (+)*

Q. *Are you a discordant person? (+)*

Q. *Is there any other point of identification? (-)*

Q. *Is there any other reason for the discordant energy on your mother? (+)*

Although the system is usually accurate, never assume that the number of reasons for the discordant energy is correct, always double-check. As you can see, there was another reason besides identification for the discordant program on his mother. Clearing the subconscious mind is often like peeling an onion, there may be another layer to remove. Some people cannot handle the energy in one large lump; the subconscious simply allows it to come up in smaller increments. When this happens, simply proceed with the next program.

Q. *What is the next reason? (a program of imprint, Chart 2)*

Q. *When was this imprint made? (pendulum indicated between 0 and 10)*

Q. *Was this imprint made between birth and age one? (+)*

Q. *Is this something you told yourself? (-)*

Q. *Who gave you the imprint? (mother, Chart 3)*

Q. *Anyone else? (father, Chart 3)*

Tony heard his father say that his mother was stupid, discordant, and negative, and he registered it as an imprint.

Q. Is there any other reason for the energy on your mother? (-)

Q. Is your mother your role model? (+)

Tony was quick to admit that he was living his life in a stupid and discordant way. He was doing a good job of fulfilling the role that was presented to him.

As I continued to work with Tony, I found he had ten percent positive and ninety-five percent discordant energy on himself. There were five reasons. They were programs of identification with his mother, benefit (of self-punishment), experience/trauma, past lives and imprint.

Here is the research done on the imprint program.

Q When was the imprint made? (40 is indicated)

Q. When you were four? (+)

Q. Is this something you told yourself? (+)

We used Chart 4 to find the energies Tony held on himself. They were hate of self, fatigue, worthlessness, stingy, withheld love, and he was guilty and deserved punishment.

Tony wanted to love himself, but he couldn't because he felt guilty, not worthy of love and deserving of punishment. His whole life was an example of acting unworthy. From a study of the picture that unfolded through Spiritual Response Therapy, it seemed evident that Tony was trying to destroy every form of his good. We will review his suicide program in Chapter 17 when we work with past lives. Although he had not committed suicide or even attempted it, he was slaying every other aspect of a successful and productive life. Once the restrictive subconscious programs were cleared, his life took a dramatic change for the better. His whole attitude changed and doors that seemed to be closed before were now open. His life became greatly enriched and ran smoother than ever before.

Tony wanted to close out his affairs in California and move to New York. To do so he needed to sell an automobile to provide money for the move. Every time he made the decision to sell, something went wrong with the vehicle. He not only had to take it off the market, but it cost him more money for repairs. Tony just couldn't seem to accumulate any money. If it wasn't the automobile costing him money, it was something else. After clearing him of the suicide program, things leveled out, the vehicle quickly sold and the means was provided to make the move.

Case study #2:   Imprint from past life
Discordant energy on mother

Tony's fiancee was so impressed with the dramatic changes in his personality and in his life that she called for counseling for herself. We began work with Ruth by clearing the discordant energy on her father, which was sixty-five percent. There were six reasons, one of which was a program of imprint.

Q. When was this imprint made? (past life, Chart 2)

She and her father were both females and good friends in that former life. There was a political situation involved and her friend (father) had betrayed her. The harm was mental and emotional and was considered serious. Further questioning revealed that she did not want to be born into this life as she was fearful that the same pain of betrayal might again be experienced. Releasing statements† were made to clear this imprint and other programs. The positive energy moved to one hundred percent and the discordant dropped to zero.

The discordant energy on her mother was only ten percent with two reasons—identification and imprint. The imprint was something she told herself at three years of age.

Q. Did you tell yourself your mother didn't love you? (+)

Q. Did you tell yourself your mother wasn't your mother any more? (This question was asked because of a conscious thought that the client had which she related to me. She said she had always felt that God was her mother) (+)

Q. Were you aware of God as your mother? (Jesus said, "And call no man your father upon the earth: for one is your Father,

---

†Since High Self can clear all programs, releasing statements are not necessary, but they can be of great benefit in certain situations, as explained in Chapter 3.

which is in heaven. [Matthew 23: 9] The client's answer was quite fascinating.

She saw God as mother and felt abandoned by her earth mother. Ruth felt her mother had withdrawn her attention from her because she was a difficult child. She also felt as if her biological mother was keeping her from going home to her real mother. When we cleared the identification and imprint, the discordant energy went to zero and the positive to one hundred. About a year later, this client wrote to me from New York.

> I must mention that my relationship with my father is finally a real relationship! No longer do I ignore him or try to put up with him. Seeing him for the first time after therapy was like seeing him with new eyes. It's been fun developing a brand new relationship with him for this past year. What a refreshing and rewarding change! For the first time in my life I feel like I really have a father. Thank you so much for your instrumental help!

Case study #3: Imprints of brain damage

One of my most fascinating cases involving imprints was with a first grader. Her mother had mentioned several times that her daughter, Angela, was having difficulty in school. Both her reading and math were far below average. Angela just could not seem to grasp either subject. I suggested that the mother bring her to me so we could find out if there were any blocks to her learning these subjects. Angela worked very well with the pendulum, and we quickly found that there were two reasons for the difficulty with math and reading—imprint and past life.

Q. *When was this imprint made? (Chart 2)*

Q. *Is this something you told yourself? (-)*

Q. *Did a doctor or nurse tell you? (+)*

Angela's mother told me that Angela was born prematurely and the doctors feared that she might have brain damage. With that knowledge as a background, the next question was asked.

Q. *Did the doctor tell you had brain damage. (+)*

Q. *Is there anything else we need to find on this imprint? (-)*

Q. *Is there another imprint? (+)*

Q. *Did this imprint occur before you were one? (+)*

Q. *Before you were six months old? (+)*

The time was determined to be near the end of her second month when she was still in the incubator. She had stopped breathing.

Q. *Is this something a doctor or nurse told you? (+)*

Q. *Did they again say they feared there might be brain damage? (+) (Now there were two messages of brain damage.)*

Q. *Do you have brain damage? (-)*

Q. *Is there anything else on this imprint? (-)*

Q. *Is there another imprint? (-)*

There was only one past life involved. Angela had been very wealthy and used her wealth to control and hurt people. She had determined that if she didn't know how to read and do math in this life, she could not become rich and thus control or hurt others. The combination of past life and imprints may sound like a simplistic way of explaining the cause of the problem, but the results obtained by removing these messages were fantastic. Before the clearing, Angela couldn't seem to add simple one-digit figures. After clearing the imprints and past life, things quickly changed. Within two weeks, Angela's mother received the following letter from her teacher.

> Dear ,
>
> Hello again! I am working with Angela on her math, and I just wanted to give you some encouraging news. Angela is doing a WONDERFUL job in math. She is working on adding two-digit numbers with SO MUCH SUCCESS! She is trying very hard and even asks to do more work than she is expected to do in class.
>
> I just wanted to let you know because I know you will be so pleased. I sure am!

Angela's mother was pleased and so was I. But that wasn't the end of it, within another three weeks, Angela brought home an official award of merit—she was on the honor role! Angela's supposed lack of intelligence because of brain damage was not keeping her from learning to do math or to read. It was the erroneous sub-conscious programs of brain damage and a negative past life that was the culprit. Had these programs not been released when they were, her life would probably have been one of constant strained effort to learn and accomplish anything of value. At least, that appears to be what has happened to many adults with whom I have worked who have had messages of brain damage.

Case study #4: Imprint of brain damage

A brain damage message was given to another client during the first year of her life. Linda had taken a tumble down a flight of stairs. One of the parents, seeing the bruised condition of the child's head, made the statement that they hoped she did not have brain damage. The incident was extremely traumatic and emotionally charged for the child and the message was received as brain damage. Clearing the message made an immediate change in Linda's life.

Case study #5: Imprints from the father Death wish

Another client's life, Katie's, was torn by emotional storms and deep depression. She had been through many hours of various kinds of counseling. She was on prescription drugs and nothing seemed to clear up her deep seated anxieties and inner conflicts.

In order to introduce her to the system, we first cleared a past life which was causing problems with her college algebra course. That situation immediately changed; she had no further trouble comprehending algebra.

Next, we began clearing the discordant energy she held on the important people in her life. The positive energy on her father was eighty percent and the discordant was one hundred. There were four imprints, all of them given to her by her father. During the first year in life, the messages received and recorded were that her father did not love her, she did not count, and she was not worthy of his love. When she was two years old, her sister was born and the message was that Katie was in the way and her father did not want her, and that he loved the new baby but not Katie. When Katie was ill at three, she received the message that her father did not care if she died. At age four, Katie had an emotional need that her father did not fulfill, and the message was that Katie was not worthy of his time and attention.

Obviously, Katie's father did not deliberately tell Katie all of these things. Her mind simply drew conclusions based on observations made through the five senses as well as the thoughts and emotions that arose from those observations. The points of identification Katie had on her father were anger, causes pain, is in pain, unemotional, unloving, uncaring, frustrated, abusive, unhappy, and cruel. She had the same energy on herself except for abusive and cruel. Katie's life was one of struggle, frustration, and lack of fulfillment although she is certainly a very talented and highly skilled person. Because of her programs of unworthiness and an underlying belief that she deserved to fail, she was doing an excellent job of frustrating her own expression of good.

Katie is another person who had a death wish. She identified with her mother, her father, her former husband, and her grandfather, all of whom she saw as having a death wish. There were also two imprints involved with the death wish.

First imprint

Q   *When was this imprint made? (birth, Chart 2)*

Q.   *Did you give yourself this imprint? (+)*

Q.   *Did you cause your mother pain? (+)*

Q.   *Do you always hurt everyone you touch? (+)*

Q.   *Did you tell yourself you didn't deserve to live? (+)*

Q.   *You should die before you cause someone else's death? (+)*

Second imprint

Q.   *When was this imprint made? (before one year of age)*

Q.   *Was this made between birth and one year of age? (+)*

Q.   *Did you tell yourself life was too painful, you wanted to die? (+)*

Q.   *Anything else on this imprint? (-)*

There were also seven past lives in which she had committed suicide. All of Katie's discordant programs were cleared and her life has made a dramatic change for the better. The habitually pained expression has left her face and her eyes light up when she smiles. She has found new employment in her previous profession as a court reporter which had caused her extreme pain and anxiety. We cleared the reasons for the pain and anxiety. Now she is completely at peace with herself and her life. She has finally determined that she is in control of her own destiny and is setting her own pace, no longer allowing herself to be pressured by others nor putting undo pressure on herself.

Case study #6: Imprints from brother

Ben had a lot of problems when he came in for therapy. His major programs seemed to be self-punishment rooted in a strong sense of inadequacy and low self-esteem. He had been on disability for several years and was diagnosed as manic-depressive. Ben was adopted as an infant and a study of his case indicated that he was aware (on a subconscious level) of his adoption. When a son was born to the adoptive parents, Ben felt very threatened by this son and over the years allowed himself to accept several limiting imprints, which have adversely affected his life.

First imprint

Q. When did this imprint take place? (age three)

Q. Is this something that your brother told you? (+)

Q. Before he was born? (+)

Q. Did he say he was going to replace you with your parents? (+)

Ben was jealous of his brother even before he was born. He was fearful that he would be replaced by his brother and that their parents would love the brother more than they did him. Obviously, these were not actually messages spoken by the unborn brother but simply the feelings raised in Ben by the impending birth.

Second imprint

Q. When was this imprint established? (age nine)

Q. Is this something your brother told you? (+)

Q. In regard to school? (+)

Q. Did he say you were lazy? (+)

Q. He intimated that you would never accomplish anything with your life? (+)

Q. Anything else on this imprint? (-)

Third imprint

Q. When was this imprint established? (age eighteen)

Q. Is this something he said about your job? (+)

Q. Did he say you would never make it as a disc-jockey? (+)

Q. Anything else? (-)

Fourth imprint

Q. When was this one made? (age five)

Q. Is this something he said? (+) (Note: Again, this was an unspoken message.)

Q. Was there jealousy involved? (+)

Q. Were you fearful your parents would love him more than they loved you? (+)

Q. Anything else we need to know? (-)

Although Ben's life has changed greatly, his process of letting go of the past and daring to step out and exercise power and dominion in his own life has been slow and is not yet fully achieved. He has found a greater sense of peace and direction in his life but has a long way to go to be completely free and productive. His patterns of restrictive behavior were too deep seated and too heavily reinforced for him to make a dramatic change in his life all at once.

Case study #7: Imprint resulting in self-punishment

Ella (case study #3 in the chapter on identification) sabotaged every relationship she'd had with a man that began to take on any depth of meaning.

She identified with her mother whom she saw as shrewish, harsh, critical, denigrating, arrogant and vindictive. She also had an imprint which she told herself at the age of four.

Q. Did you tell yourself that your father and mother could not be trusted and you weren't going to care anymore? (+) (She couldn't trust herself in a relationship.)

Q. Since your father and mother have a poor relationship, you believe you will also? (+)

Q. Did you tell yourself life wasn't worth trying to live effectively? (+)

Q. Did your father pay more attention to other little girls? (+)

Q. Did he make you feel unworthy of his love? (+)

Q. Did you feel guilty because you didn't love your father and mother? (We had previ-

ously confirmed that she did not love them.)
(+)

Q. *Do you, therefore, feel unworthy of any good in your own life? (+)*

Q. *Could you ever please your parents? (-)*

Q. *Could you ever please someone else? (-)*

There was more information that came forth before we were finished researching this imprint program. She had had a desire to hurt a baby when she was a child because of jealousy. She put her mouth over the spout of a teapot as a form of self-punishment for being jealous of the baby and for which her parents severely punished her. These factors, and a number of others, all contributed to Ella's strong program of self-punishment which destroyed any meaningful relationship with a man, or for that matter anything beneficial in her life.

CHAPTER 12

Experience/Trauma
ဆ ရ

Traumatic experiences can have far reaching effects on your life. Everyone has some discordant things happen to them during the course of their life. How they affect you is determined by factors such as your age at the time of the happening, whether you have high or low self-esteem, how centered and at peace you are, the support or lack of support by family and/or friends, personal awareness of the meaning of life, and other circumstances. Like other programs, experience/trauma may go back to birth or even before. Regardless of the time frame, traumatic experiences can have a very discordant and profound influence on a person's current life expression.

Childhood Trauma

It never ceases to amaze me how the interactions between parents and their child during the child's formative years can have such a profound effect on the rest of the child's life. Even more amazing is that many of the programs, although tucked away from view in the subconscious mind with no conscious knowledge of them, are often destructive and limiting. Parents do not intentionally establish destructive or limiting programs in their children nor are they aware that there is such a possibility. The programs become destructive because under the emotional stress of childhood, the rational mind is shunted aside by the strong feelings. Thus the messages are not received in the form they are sent. Rather, a discordant meaning is given to them which then negatively affects the person's life.

I believe the factor that causes a program to be set up in the subconscious mind is not so much the event itself but the amount of emo-

tional energy attached to it. When you are a child, you are easily moved by your emotions, and programs are quickly and easily established in the subconscious mind. When you are an adult, you are more in charge of your emotions (or at least you should be) and can easily recognize that you do not have to put a discordant connotation on things that happen in your life. When you become an adult, you have the opportunity to look at things in a new light and put away childish ways of thinking, feeling, and doing.

Spiritual Response Therapy is a marvelous, accurate, and powerful way of getting in touch with the childhood programs that are causing hurt and removing them from the subconscious mind. It is the way you, as an adult, can build new programs into the subconscious mind that will set you free from childish beliefs, perceptions, and judgments. Patient and exacting work is required. However, the benefits are fantastic and well worth the time and effort.

Sexual abuse

Traumatic experiences rooted in the area of sexual molestation are one of the few events I have found to cause the subconscious to deliberately lie. One person had a reason of trauma for the one hundred percent discordant energy on his father. When we started trying to pinpoint the energy, the pendulum gave erratic responses. Sensing that the subconscious mind might be trying to cover up sexual molestation, I asked my High Self (the inner superconscious mind) if that was the reason and received a "yes" response. I returned to working directly with the client and received the following answers.

Q. *Is the trauma sexual molestation? (-)*

Q. *Is there a reason of trauma? (-)*

Q. *Is there any reason for the discordant energy on your father? (-)*

Q. *Is there any discordant energy on your father? (-)*

Considerable time was spent using releasing statements to erase the heavy fear of revealing the truth before the subconscious responses began to make sense and the truth of the sexual molestation was admitted.

Many times the molestation may occur repeatedly over an extended period of time, even years, and the person will have no conscious memory of it. The trauma is so great that it is completely erased from the conscious mind. Resistance may be encountered when working with any of the programs but more often when sexual molestation is involved. The subconscious may move the pendulum in a circle, at an angle or simply not move at all in an attempt to avoid answering the question. The original experience was distressing and painful and the subconscious was seeking to protect the person from having to go through the pain again.

Although the pain experienced with Spiritual Response Therapy is a small fraction of that experienced with most other forms of counseling, the therapist must make every effort to exercise good judgment and caution to prepare the client for the experience and to protect them as much as possible from the pain. Even then the inner mind will sometimes seek to hide information. This resistance may be released by assuring the subconscious mind that it is now okay to reveal the answer. When this happens, simply make the following statements and have the client repeat them after you. "I release all fear of answering the question." "I release all resistance to the answer." "I give the subconscious permission to answer the question."

If you sense that the person is trying to protect the honor of themselves or of someone else, have them say, "There is no judgment, criticism, condemnation, or punishment. There is only a desire to know the truth and to be free.

Answer the question." Then ask the question again. Usually, after making the releasing statements, the subconscious will answer with a "yes" or "no" movement of the pendulum. If you continue to get a blocking movement, have the client repeat the releasing statements again. Go through the process repeatedly until the subconscious answers.

Technique

To research experience/trauma programs, use the standard technique as explained in Chapter 7. I never search for details about causes of a particular message recorded in the subconscious mind. I simply obtain the basic message so it may be cleared. Usually a lot of details are not needed in order to clear the discordant energy thereby saving time for more productive work.

**Case study #1: Past life suicide
                  Traumatic experiences with
                  women**

Here is an example of how the trauma experienced in past lives has strongly influenced the present life. Working with Andy was not always easy, but it was certainly fascinating. The discordant energy on everyone and everything we researched always had its roots in past lives. Andy was male in almost every past life we researched. This does not happen very often. Usually clients have a fairly even mix between male and female incarnations. Life was pretty difficult for Andy. Shortly before he came to see me he had gone to a store to purchase a shotgun with the intent to commit suicide.

Q. *Do you have a desire to kill yourself? (+)*

Q. *What is the area? (past lives, Chart 2)*

Q. *How many past lives are involved? (Eight)*

The past lives had a basic theme running through them with only minor variations. Andy was male in every past life. There was always a woman involved with whom he had a strong emotional attachment. She was invariably stolen by another man. Every life ended with Andy killing both of them and then committing suicide.

Q. *Is there any other reason for the desire to commit suicide? (-)*

We made the necessary releasing statements†
to release the energy of these past lives and
checked to make certain they were clear.

Q. *Do you have a desire to kill yourself? (+)*

Q. *Is the energy on these eight past lives
dissolved? (+)*

Q. *Is there any reason for you to desire to kill
yourself? (+)*

Q. *What is the reason? (past lives)*

Q. *How many past lives are there? (Eight)*

Q. *Are these eight other lives rather than the
same eight we have already cleared? (+)*

Q. *Are these carbon copies of the lives we have
already looked at and cleared? (+)*

Q. *Can we clear them without finding all of
the particulars of each life? (+)*

We spent two sessions working on these past
lives and clearing the desire that Andy had to
kill himself. Although all of this deals with past
life energies, it was programs of experience/
trauma that were having far reaching conse-
quences in this life. Fortunately, Andy made
the conscious decision not to do away with
himself in this life. When a person has committed suicide in past lives, it seems as though
they must face and overcome the desire to do
so again in a subsequent life. Unless these
discordant patterns are dissolved, they will
continue to exert pressure on the soul until
they are faced and overcome. "Him that
overcometh will I make a pillar in the temple of
my God, and he shall go no more out..." (Revelation, 3:12).

Andy's mother, father, and many others in his
present life were involved with him in previous
lives where they often caused him pain and
anguish and often death. He had a strong
sexual attraction in this life toward his mother
and it was causing him a lot of fear and emotional trauma. This also carried over from past
lives where she had been his wife and had
caused him injury and death several times.
Over and over we found past lives where the
women involved caused him great trauma.
However, not until our last session together did
we find the source of the problem. We were
working on why he had difficulty with every
female relationship.

Q. *Are you fearful of women? (+)*

Q. *How many reasons are there? (One)*

Q. *What is the reason? (Past lives)*

Q. *What were you? (female)*

Andy, then a young woman of thirteen, was
just entering puberty. He had been mentally
and emotionally abused by a group of women.
They physically raped and tortured him and
burned him alive. This was a very heavy experience of trauma for Andy.

Q. *Are women to be feared and avoided? (+)*

Q. *Do women have total control over you? (+)*

Q. *Must you suffer at their hands? (+)*

Q. *For your own safety, must you break off
relationships with women before they can
harm you? (+)*

Q. *Must you do so quickly? (+)*

Having traumatic experiences with women was
the major theme that controlled Andy's life
from beginning to end. He made the following
statements to me, when we had cleared much
of his discordant programming, "I finally
understand why my relations with all of the
women in my life have been so chaotic and
unfulfilling. I feel better now. I am so glad I
have gotten rid of the desire to commit suicide."

**Case study #2:   Sexual trauma
            Fear of success
            Trauma resulting from father's
            death**

Jack was another client who's current problems
had their roots in programs of experience/
trauma from past lives. I found that the past
lives often had sexual connotations and it
became very obvious that much of the same
energy was surfacing in this life. Jack came in
for counseling because he wanted to release his
fear of urinating in a public restroom which
was causing him a great deal of emotional pain
in this life.

One of his past lives was in Japan where he
caused himself pain and death because of his
sexual fantasies. He circumcised himself,
causing an infection that led to his death.
Another past life found Jack with the woman
who is his wife now. She was a prostitute in

---

†Since High Self can clear all programs, releasing statements are not necessary, but they can be of great benefit in certain situations, as explained in Chapter 3.

that life. He contracted venereal disease from her and underwent a lot of personal ridicule and emotional pain in that life. Both of these past lives were major causes of the pain and limitation Jack was experiencing in this life.

A third past life was also involved in his current life problem. He and another person in that past life were caught in mutual masturbation, put in stocks and held up to public humiliation. In the current life, he was caught urinating in public by the lady next door. He was in the back yard and the next door neighbor happened to look over the fence and see him. He was only a child, but the incident triggered the past life trauma of public ridicule.

In another past life, he, as a male, had oral sex with a female who "bit it off." The traumatic past life program was strongly reinforced in the present life at eight years of age when he was forced into oral sex by some older boys. He was also forced to expose himself in front of several of his peers.

Jack had a fear of success program in his subconscious mind. As a construction worker and contractor, he had not taken work that would lead to employing other people. All of the work on every job was done by himself. Also, he has talent as a designer and graphic artist but had been fearful of using it in any way other than for his own satisfaction. His fear of success was associated with events in a past life involving identification and trauma programs.

There were several people involved with the past life who have come together again in this one. Jack was a female designer then and his present wife was the husband. Jack's father in the current life was their female child then. I was in that life as a promoter-builder. My wife then is my wife now. Jack had designed a bridge. I convinced him that it was a sound design and used the plans to start construction. One of the reasons Jack consented was because his daughter needed an operation and the profit was to provide the necessary funds for the surgeon. The bridge collapsed while under construction and both Jack's husband (wife in this life) and I were killed. The daughter never received the operation. My wife blamed Jack for my death and created great difficulties for him. Although Jack had never met me or my wife prior to his first counseling

session, he stated that he was holding discordant energy on both of us.

Jack's father died when Jack was eleven and the father's death was another reason of trauma causing Jack to limit his success. His father was an alcoholic and Jack had a subconscious belief that his father's death through alcohol was a result of the pressures of trying to be a success.

Q. *Are you fearful that if you are successful you will destroy your own life? (+)*

Q. *If you are successful, will you become an alcoholic like your father? (+)*

Q. *Were you responsible for his death? (+)*

Q. *Are you trying to fulfill his unfinished life? (+)*

Q. *Was your father a failure? (+)*

Q. *Are you trying to take his place? (+)*

Q. *Was your mother cold and uncaring about your father's death? (+)*

Q. *Is there any other energy on this trauma that we need to find? (-)*

Jack also identified with his father's personality traits of being inconsistent, confused, unfulfilled, and failing to fulfill his potential. Although he saw his father as irresponsible and alcoholic, he did not identify himself with those character traits. The fear of success program, the sexual fantasizing and the fear of urinating in a public restroom were greatly relieved by the time Jack and I had finished our counseling sessions. He was also free of the discordant energy he had held on my wife and me.

Case study #3: Past life trauma causing fear of success

Tim, a real estate salesman, was another client who feared success based on trauma from a past life.

Q. *What were you? (male)*

Q. *Any one else involved? (group)*

Q. *Were you in a position of leadership? (+, military leader)*

Q. *Were you successful? (+)*

Q. *Were you a failure? (+)*

Q. *Were your failures greater than your successes? (+)*

Q. *Is that the reason for the problem now? (-)*

Q. Is the reason for the problem now, because there was a final defeat? (+)

Q. Are you failing now so that you will not suffer a final defeat? (+)

Q. Anything else we need to know in order to clear the discordant energy? (-)

Tim listed more property in the thirty days after we cleared this program than he had in the previous year!

Case study #4: Trauma of childhood sexual abuse
Trauma with step-daughter

Katie had one hundred percent discordant energy on her father with programs of identification, benefit, conflict, organ language, self-punishment, four imprint programs and five experience/trauma programs. After considerable questioning, Katie's subconscious revealed that her father had sexually molested her from infancy through her sixth year and physically abused her when she was eight and nine. This horrendous beginning had left its mark.

Katie was divorced and separated by distance from her former husband and her stepdaughter. The discordant energy on the step-daughter was high due to several programs: self-punishment, identification, and trauma with three subprograms, one of which was involved with a past life. Because Katie felt like she had deserted her stepdaughter when the girl needed her badly, self-punishment held the strongest discordant energy. Trauma was next. After a short conversation about their relationship, we found the following.

Trauma number one:

Q. You had a desire to drown her? (+)

Q. Any other reason for the trauma? (-)

Trauma number two:

Q. This took place on her seventh birthday? (+)

Q. She called you on the phone? (+)

Q. Were you upset because you couldn't be there to help her celebrate? (+)

Q. Any thing else we need to know? (-)

Trauma number three:

Q. When was this established? (past life)

Q. What were you? (female)

Q. What was she? (daughter)

Q. Did she drown in that life? (+)

Q. Did you deliberately drown her? (+)

Q. Did you drown her because she was deformed? (+)

Q. Anything else we need to know about this past life trauma? (-)

The energy of drowning and the guilt attached needed to be faced and overcome in this life. Many times it appears that the past life energies are being met and opportunities being presented to "do it differently this time around."

Case study #5: Trauma caused by father's failure to protect

Deborah had discordant energy on her father because, in her opinion, he always treated her badly. There was a past life in which he died when she was five which left her feeling rejected and hurt. The experience of trauma in the current life took place when Deborah was four. The following questions were based on her conscious memory of the events.

Q. Did your father punish you? (+)

Q. Did he spank you? (+)

Q. Were you upset because it was so unusual for him to punish you in any way? (+)

Q. He laughed at you when the turkey chased you? (+)

Q. Were you in danger? (+)

Q. Did your father refuse to protect you? (+)

Q. Was this a form of abandonment by your father? (+)

From a parent's point of view the incident with the turkey could have been amusing. However, from a child's point of view the turkey was an attacking monster to be greatly feared. The parent did not fulfill the role of protector and deliverer but abandoned her to her fate of injury or even death. This was consistent with the past life experience in which her father abandoned her by his own death. He simply was no longer there to care for, protect, and raise her. What made it all the more important was that she saw him as a very loving, supportive person who in her greatest time of need, when her very life was threatened, failed her.

Case study #6:   Sexual molestation

Dawn had one hundred percent discordant and zero positive energy on her brother. The greatest amount of discordant energy was held because of an incident when she was fourteen.

Q.   He tried to molest you? (+)

Other reasons of trauma were:

Q.   The rape he was involved in? (+)

Q.   From having to visit him in jail? (+)

Q.   The trauma of seeing him hurt your parents? (+)

Q.   He embarrassed you by his actions in front of others? (+)

Case study #7:   Fear of success
Self-destruction

Many people have fear of success programs, but Sue had so many we could not determine the number. We simply started work without knowing how many there were. Additional programs were uncovered as we went along. Sue had a strong self-destruct program that led to her failure to express her life in a productive manner. One of the first to be uncovered was a reason of trauma originating in the womb.

Q   Did you cause your mother pain? (+)

Q.   Did she have problems carrying you? (+)

Q.   Did you want to be born? (-)

Q.   Were you trying to abort yourself? (+)

Q.   Did you fail to abort yourself? (+)

Q.   Must you suffer now because you failed to abort? (+)

Q.   Must you suffer by being a failure now? (+)

Sue's self-destruct and failure programs were very deeply embedded, many resulting from unpleasant former lives. She had spent many hours counseling with other professional counselors before coming to me. When she first started Spiritual Response Therapy, we spent considerable time removing subconscious blocks to using a pendulum (see Chapter 8) before the system would work. After our first two hours of work, I apologized to Sue for accomplishing so little. Her statement to me was, "Are you kidding! You have accomplished more, and helped me more in two hours, than in all of the many hours spent in other forms of therapy." Sue's life has taken a dramatic turn for the better. She has new employment and other areas of her life have improved immensely, bringing her joy and peace.

Case study #8:   Self-destruction

In the majority of my cases, birth is considered a traumatic experience and self-destruct and self-punishment programs are often established at that time. Netta had committed suicide in three past lives. From birth, she had a sense that she was not valuable or worthwhile and must punish and destroy herself. Her life's challenge was to overcome the past life suicide program in order to be free.

Q.   Did you cause your mother physical and emotional pain at birth? (+)

Q.   Because she wanted a boy? (+)

Q.   Does that mean you are not valuable as a woman? (+)

Q.   Since you are worthless, must you destroy yourself mentally, emotionally and physically? (+)

As described in the chapter on identification, Netta had sixteen reasons to punish herself. After her programs were cleared, her life changed dramatically for the better.

Case study #9:   Rebellion against authority

Lynn resented anyone trying to control her. Shirking her responsibilities was a way of saying, "You can't tell me what to do." There were four programs involving trauma that caused the rebellion against authority.

Trauma number one:

Q.   How old were you? (three)

Q.   Your father spanked you for disobedience? (Saying no to a direct instruction.) (+)

Q.   Are you rebelling against authority by shirking the responsibility of following direct instructions? (+)

Trauma number two:

Q.   How old were you? (eight)

Q.   Were you rebelling against the church school? (+)

Trauma number three:

Lynn was sixteen and wanted to start dating. She felt her mother was trying to control her and restrict her dating.

Trauma number four:

Lynn had been working in a store at the time this trauma was established. She made incorrect change for a customer and believed she was incapable of handling any employment.

Not only have Lynn's inner programs been changed, her outer actions have changed also. She is handling her employment very well and even her relationship with her intimate other has improved and many of the tensions between them eliminated.

Case study #10: Irrational self-punishment programs

While working on the discordant energy Fred had on his parents, we found a lot of seemingly irrational programs. The first trauma program caused Fred to hold discordant energy on his mother.

Q. *When was this trauma experienced?* (birth)

Q. *Were you afraid of being born?* (+)

Q. *Anything else we need to find on this trauma?* (-)

Another traumatic experience was registered between six and nine months of age.

Q. *Were you frightened by your father?* (+)

Q. *Did he spank you?* (+)

Q. *Did that register as physical abuse?* (+)

Q. *Did your mother fail to protect you from your father?* (+)

Q. *Anything else we need to find on this trauma?* (-)

Fred registered several imprint programs with regard to his mother. At five years of age, he told himself that he did not love his mother because she failed to protect him against his father and against life. The following year his mother slighted his ability to learn and promote his own well being. She told him he was not trying hard enough. In later years, she told him that when he grew up he would either be in prison or in the insane asylum. Fred's subconscious mind accepted these statements as truth.

Q. *Are you potential prison material?* (+)

Q. *Are you potential asylum material?* (+)

Fred liked to punish himself, or so it seemed. This desire to punish himself came from his experience with his father. The following beliefs were registered when Fred was seven years old and his father started whipping him with a belt.

Q. *Did he punish you unjustly?* (+)

Q. *Was he afraid of you?* (+)

Q. *Did your father love you?* (+)

Q. *Did your father like you?* (-)

Q. *Does mental, emotional and physical abuse make you worthwhile and likable?* (+)

Q. *Do you set yourself up for mental, emotional, and physical abuse so you can feel worthwhile?* (+)

When Fred was two years of age, he suffered a head injury. Although it was not a serious injury, it was traumatic for him and some destructive messages were recorded in the subconscious mind.

Q. *Did you have an injury?* (+)

Q. *Was it a head injury?* (+)

Q. *Is there a message involved that causes headaches?* (+)

Q. *Is the injury a cause of your headaches now?* (+)

Q. *Something in regard to the parents causing you to punish yourself now by having headaches?* (+)

Q. *Are the headaches and sinus a way of punishing your parents?* (+)

Q. *Because your parents didn't take good care of you and protect you from injury?* (+)

Q. *Is there anything else we need to find on this reason of trauma?* (-)

This example shows how the mind is not always rational in its programming. Fred thought he was punishing his parents by having headaches and sinus problems and he was only hurting himself.

Q. *Is there another reason of trauma?* (+)

Fred fell and cut his neck when he was four. This happened when he was doing something he should not have been doing.

Q. *Was this program established when you fell and cut your neck?* (+)

Q. *Any self-punishment involved in this?* (+)

Q. *Are you punishing yourself now by having headaches and sinus?* (+)

Q. *When you do things you know or believe you should not do, do you always need to punish yourself by having headaches and or sinus problems?* (+)

Q. *Have you done or are you doing something your parents would not approve of?* (+)

Q. *Are you having physical pain because of doing something your parents would not approve of now?* (+)

Q. *Must you justify all your actions based on your parents mores and standards?* (+)

Q. *Any other reason for the headaches?* (-)

Fred's headaches and sinus problems were based on his desire to punish himself for what he considered wrong actions and on his desire to punish his parents for not taking good care of him. One of his reasons for self-punishment, was that he and Lynn were living together. Fred is now free from headaches and sinus problems. Since he does not have to set himself up for headaches as a means of self-punishment for living with Lynn out of wedlock, they have decided to get married. Of course, there were other programs both of them had that needed to be cleared before they were ready to deepen their relationship.

CHAPTER 13

Benefit
ဆ ငာ

Have you ever gone to Las Vegas or Reno and visited one of the casinos hoping to strike it rich? How was the pay-off? Did you win a lot or a little, or did you drop a bundle? Any way you look at it, regardless of which side of the ledger you were on, there was a pay-off. You may not have been on the winning end, but there was a pay-off. Benefits are like that. They can be a credit to us, bringing a beneficial result or they can cause us to be a loser bringing difficulty, pain, poverty, sickness, and even death. Suicide can appear to be a benefit for the person who is experiencing unbearable emotional trauma or physical pain. However, suicide is not a good way to leave the physical body.

Technique

There is a logical process to follow when using Spiritual Response Therapy that can save a lot of back-tracking and extra work. Suppose there are four reasons for a problem: programs of trauma, benefit, identification, and imprint. In the order given, the first program (trauma) would have the highest discordant charge and the last one given (imprint) would have the smallest discordant charge. Regardless of which program is given first, you always start with identification if it is listed as one of the programs. Next research the imprint program, if it is given as one of the reasons. After that investigate the trauma program. Only then would you research the benefit program. This order can save a lot of work simply because the benefit usually has its roots in the identification, imprint, and trauma programs.

One of the best ways to focus on a reason of benefit is to find the time of life when the benefit was established. Once the time frame has been determined, questions can be related to the circumstances that existed then. It is astounding just how many problems stem from the messages that people are given by others or themselves at the time of birth or soon thereafter.

When clearing the discordant energy of a benefit program, it is not always necessary to make releasing statements[†] to specifically clear the benefit if it has its roots in identification, imprint, past lives, etc. You simply make the necessary statements to release the other programs and usually the benefit program is dissolved also. After the releasing statements are completed, check to make certain the discordant energy has been completely dissolved.

The subconscious mind is extremely powerful. When you understand this power and how to work with the inner mind in a positive, constructive way, there is no limit to what you may become or accomplish in life. Using it correctly is extremely important. If you use it in the wrong way, you will suffer because the subconscious mind is just as efficient and quick at producing a discordant program as it is a positive one.

To research benefit programs:

1. If there are other programs related to the benefit program, research them in the proper order (identification, imprint, experi-

---

†Since High Self can clear all programs, releasing statements are not necessary, but they can be of great benefit in certain situations, as explained in Chapter 3.

ence/trauma) before researching the benefit program.

2. Once the research work has been completed on the first three programs, ask:

Q. *Is there any reason of benefit other than that involved with the identification, imprint and trauma programs?*

Further questioning is not necessary unless a "yes" answer has been received.

3. Determine what the benefit is. (Self-punishment may be involved.)

4. Ask when the benefit program was established.

5. Determine the circumstances.

6. Ask High Self if the program can be cleared.

7. Ask High Self to clear the program.

8. Once the program is cleared, return to the questioning process:

Q. *Is there another program to research and clear?*

Case study #1: Discordant energy on God

Ella had discordant energy on God. She identified God with her mother, father, brother, grandmother, and two aunts. There was also an imprint in which she told herself that God did not love her or take care of her, God wanted to punish her because she sinned, she deserved to be limited, she did not deserve God's love, and she was incapable of winning His love. There was also a traumatic experience involved in which much of this energy was reinforced.

Q. *Is there any reason of benefit other than the ones involved with the identification, imprint, and trauma? (+, self-punishment)*

Q. *Are all of the points of identification, imprint, and trauma involved with a benefit of self-punishment? (+)*

Q. *Is there anything else we are looking for on this benefit? (-)*

As you can see, it would have taken a long time to find all of the reasons for a pay-off of self-punishment. As explained in the Technique section of this chapter, following this order of investigation eliminates going over the same ground again and again. When the releasing

statements are made on the identification, imprint and trauma, the benefit will automatically clear.

Case study # 2: Fear of mental illness

Phil had always been fearful that he might, if he were not extremely careful, be mentally out of control. This fear had its roots in an experience as an early teen. During his teen years, he experienced a lot of emotional strain in his life and sometimes felt like he was losing control of his mind. One day when the emotional stress seemed to be more than Phil could stand, he feared that he was about to go crazy. His mother came to his aid and was able to calm him down by spending a lot of time with him. However, Phil was greatly upset by this incident, and the fear of going out of his mind haunted him for many years.

Some years later, when Phil was driving a vehicle with a leaking exhaust, he got a very severe headache from breathing the fumes. He found that his total concentration was on the headache. For the first time in many years, Phil felt like he was completely in control of his own mind—there was no room for uncontrolled thoughts. Investigating why he had headaches, we found he had programmed and reinforced this response. Driving or riding in a motor vehicle had become the stimulus for a discordant response, a headache. The programs were imprint and benefit.

Imprint:

Q. *Is this imprint something you told yourself? (+)*

Q. *Do you need to punish yourself for disconnecting the smog control? (+)*

Q. *Is it wrong to even drive a vehicle because the emissions will cause air pollution? (+)*

Q. *Do you tell yourself every time you ride in a motor vehicle you are to get a headache? (+)*

Q. *Do you deserve to be punished when you ride in a motor vehicle? (+)*

Q. *Is there a spiritual lesson to be learned through headaches? (+)*

Q. *Is the lesson that headaches help you to concentrate? (+)*

Q. *Do they put you in charge mentally, emotionally, physically, and spiritually? (+)*

Q. *Did you tell yourself headaches would help you control your mind and help you stop worrying? (+)*

Q. *Did you tell yourself that having a headache is a sure way to be in control of your mind? (+)*

Q. *Did you tell yourself that having headaches will keep you from going insane? (+)*

Benefit:

Q. *Do you get to punish yourself for disconnecting the smog control and contributing to pollution? (+)*

Q. *Does having headaches give you the benefit of being in control of your own thoughts and emotions? (+)*

Q. *Do headaches prove you are in control? (+)*

Q. *Does having headaches keep you from going insane? (+)*

Q. *Any other reason for the headaches? (-)*

Further questioning revealed that the subconscious mind used the circumstances of the faulty exhaust and the resultant headaches to free Phil of his intense fear of losing his mind. The headaches were a constant reminder that he had control. Unfortunately, in Phil's case, one discordant, fear-ridden program was replaced with another one just as harmful.

Case study #3: Fear of living

Katie (Case study #5 in Chapter 11 Imprints) was a highly skilled court reporter who was much in demand. However, she found that she could not work as a court reporter because it caused extreme emotional pressure and she feared for her sanity. The first reason for the problem was an identification program in which she saw her father as being very fearful of life. The second reason was an imprint program she gave herself at birth by telling herself life was fearful, painful and difficult. When we researched the third reason, a benefit program, we found that it was blocking her prosperity.

Q. *Is there any reason for the benefit other than what is involved with the identification and imprint programs? (+)*

Q. *Do you believe you do not deserve to prosper through holding a good job because you caused your mother pain at birth? (+)*

Q. *Are you using fear as a tool to help you fail and to keep yourself from being productive? (+)*

Q. *Any other benefit involved? (-)*

Case study #4: Blocks to prosperity

While working with Beth on prosperity, we found that there were eighteen programs causing her to block her own prosperity.

Q. *Do you believe you have the right to prosper? (-)*

Q. *Do you believe God wants you to prosper? (-)*

Q. *Is there a program of benefit? (+)*

Q. *Is the benefit that you get to punish yourself? (+)*

Q. *When was this established? (birth)*

Q. *Because you caused your mother pain at birth? (+)*

Q. *Because you caused your family financial difficulties? (+)*

Q. *Was it wrong for you to be conceived? (+)*

Q. *Is there any other program of benefit? (-)*

Case study #5: Difficulty losing weight

Sometimes the weave of a person's programs is so convoluted that one aspect conflicts with another. Iris had considerable difficulty losing weight. The following is what we found on using sugar and eating sweets.

Q. *Do you still have a problem with sugar? (+)*

Q. *How many reasons are there? (2)*

Q. *What is one of the areas? (Conflict program)*

Q. *What is the other area? (Benefit program)*

We found we could not separate the conflict from the benefit in this problem—these two programs worked in tandem.

Q. *Does eating sugar give you immediate energy? (+)*

Q. *Does it give you immediate satisfaction? (+)*

Q. *Does it make you temporarily feel better? (+)*

Q. *In order to live a good life, must you be sweet? (+)*

Q. *In order to be a channel of light, must you be sweet? (+)*

Q. *Are little girls sugar and spice and every-thing nice? (+) (Conflict: She must eat sugar to be little.)*

Q. *You have a compulsion to eat a lot of sweets? (+)*

Q. *Are eating sugar and drinking alcohol ways to give yourself love? (+) (It was also a way to get approval, reward, and positive strokes.)*

Q. *Is there any other reason for eating sugar and sweets? (-)*

Iris wanted desperately to be free from the compulsion to eat sweets so she could become slim and trim. The desire to be slim and trim was in conflict with the benefit of being nice, sweet, energized, a channel of light and receiving the strokes and self love she desired.

Iris also had high discordant energy on a friend. In past lives, they both were Israelite soldiers at the time of Jesus. My client had been in favor of Jesus' crucifixion and felt she was responsible for his death. Her friend was a follower of Jesus and did not wish to see him crucified. There was conflict between them regarding Jesus and his ministry and it was surfacing as an undercurrent in this life caus-ing mixed emotions and discordant results in their relationship.

Q. *Are you in conflict over an understanding of Jesus? (+)*

Q. *Are both of you failing to express your spiritual beauty? (+)*

Q. *Is she failing to express her spiritual poten-tial? (+)*

Q. *Are you failing to express your spiritual potential? (+)*

Q. *Are you justified in holding discordant energy on her because she is failing to be spiritual? (+)*

Q. *Are you more spiritual than she is? (+)*

Q. *Is there any other program of benefit? (-)*

Case study #6: Distrust of God

Owen had zero positive and one hundred percent discordant energy on God with fifteen reasons. He was identifying God with five family members all of whom he saw as spiritu-ally confused, spiritually hypocritical, and "fouled up" by God. He was in conflict because God had upset the whole family and concluded that God was not to be trusted. There were also seven past lives in which he believed that God caused the death of himself or loved ones. After clearing these programs, we asked the following questions.

Q. *Is there any program of identification to hold discordant energy on God? (-)*

Q. *Any program of imprint? (-)*

Q. *Any program of self-punishment? (-)*

Q. *Any program of past lives? (-)*

Q. *Any program of benefit? (-)*

Q. *Any program of any kind to hold discor-dant energy on God? (-)*

Q. *Is the discordant energy now zero? (+)*

Q. *Is the positive energy now one hundred percent? (+)*

Instead of asking "yes/no" questions about the positive/discordant energy, you could use one of the charts with numbers around the wheel.

Q. *What is the discordant energy on God? (zero)*

Q. *What is the positive energy on God? (100%)*

CHAPTER 14

Conflict

ℰᏜ ᏟᏅ

The sources of conflict are endless. Any time a desire collides with a "cannot," there is a conflict. Any time a desire is met with a lack of worthiness, there is a conflict. Conflict takes many forms and often has its roots running back to early childhood and even into past lives. A conflict program can originally be established at a conscious level, but may later be repressed and become a "below the surface" program in the subconscious mind.

Another type of conflict is a conscious desire that is offset by a previously established taboo. These taboos may have their source in this life or in past lives. They may be expressed verbally as: "No! That is wrong." "You can't." "You mustn't." "You shouldn't." "It just isn't done!" "It just isn't proper for someone like you/us."

Conflict may be a source of strong guilt which can cause programs of self-punishment. If you have such programs you may inflict mental, emotional, or even physical pain on yourself. Many people are completely unaware of the source of conflict in their life since they have repressed the awareness of the causes.

Technique

To research conflict programs, use the standard procedure as explained in Chapter 7. Conflict programs are not always as clear cut and readily determinable as some of the other programs such as identification, imprint, and trauma. However, the discordant energy due to a conflict program clears just as quickly and easily as does the energy of any other program. You simply make the releasing statements† and

then check to make certain all of the energy is depleted and that the new programs have been successfully entered into the subconscious mind.

Case study #1:   Desire for a meaningful life

Ella had a lot of heavy discordant messages from other members of her family. Her father repeatedly whipped her with a belt in an attempt to force her to learn to tie her shoes. He compared her to a neighbor boy, saying she was dumb and stupid because the little boy could tie his shoes and she could not. Her father would demonstrate how to tie her shoes and then have her try. When she failed to tie them properly, he whipped her. This happened again and again which strongly reinforced her feeling of stupidity and unworthiness.

The family had a pickup truck and Ella was forced to ride in the back of the truck even in inclement weather because she was not good enough to sit in front with the family. Her brother would call her stupid, dumb and anything else that came to mind and tell her she wasn't good enough to sit up front with the rest of them. Ella's brother was never corrected or called to task for the things he said to her. Ella grew up with a lot of conscious and subconscious messages that she was worthless, stupid, and incapable of ever doing anything worthwhile in her life.

Ella wanted to feel good about life and about herself. However, her desire for a meaningful life was in complete conflict with her subconscious programs. She had sixteen reasons for

---

†Since High Self can clear all programs, releasing statements are not necessary, but they can be of great benefit in certain situations, as explained in Chapter 3.

holding one hundred percent discordant energy on herself. One of the reasons was an identification with her father in which she saw him as an S.O.B., undemonstrative, unloving, demanding, always wrong, judgmental, and having low self-esteem.

She derived benefit because the "unworthy" programs fulfilled her desire to feel guilty. She felt guilty because she made a mess of her life. The more she "messed up," the more guilty she felt. It became a self-fulfilling prophesy. She was programmed to make a mess of her life because that was the way she received her discordant strokes which was the only kind of stroking she had ever received from her family.

Although Ella wanted to express her life in a positive way, she was in conflict with her desire to earn the love and respect of her father and other family members. The only way she could do that was to become like them and take on all of their discordant traits. Ella became a closed, retiring person who was afraid to be around people because she considered herself unworthy of attention, respect or love. One of her basic subconscious messages was that she should never have been born. She felt she simply was not worthy of living and becoming someone of value in life. This is how our research of the conflict program unfolded:

Q. *If you loved yourself, would you be okay? (+)*

Q. *Can you be okay? (-)*

Q. *If you loved yourself, would that make your parents wrong? (+)*

Q. *Would you lose your parents love if you loved yourself? (+)*

Q. *Is that why you are in conflict with wanting to be all right? You would lose your parents love? (+)*

Q. *Would you lose your identity with your father who is your role model? (+)*

Q. *Was it wrong for you to be born? (+)*

Q. *Since you chose to be born can you ever be worthwhile? (-)*

Q. *Must you always live your life in such a way as to prove you are unworthy, stupid, and incapable? (+)*

Q. *Is there any other reason of conflict? (-)*

Ella's desire to be something more in life was in direct conflict with her childhood programs.

With these inner conflicts there was simply no way she could break out of the old mold her family had helped create.

Later, after a lot of clearing work, Ella decided she would take some college courses to further her limited education. Once, when her test papers were returned, she approached her instructor and informed her that she must have made a mistake in grading her paper, she could not possibly have performed well enough to qualify for such a high score on the test. The instructor had a difficult time convincing Ella that she had actually earned the grade given.

Ella also had eight reasons for holding one hundred percent discordant energy on God. She identified God with her mother, father, brother and two aunts. The list of adjectives included manipulative, undemonstrative, unloving, perfectionist, demanding, vindictive, always wrong, cruel, controlling, etc. The imprints that she gave herself were: "God does not love me and does not take care of me. God wants to punish me because I sin. I do not deserve His love and I do deserve to be limited. I am incapable of winning His love." She wanted to experience a good relationship with God but felt she did not deserve good. She felt that if she was unable to please her family, she could never please God.

Ella hated house cleaning with a passion and was the first to admit her house was a mess. She identified with her aunt in many ways including the aunt's keeping a messy house. Ella was punishing herself for having a cluttered house by having to live in that cluttered house. Here is a program that exemplifies self-punishment, benefit, and conflict. It is so involved that there is no way to isolate the individual parts.

Q. *If you clean house, can you punish yourself? (-)*

Q. *If you clean house, does it mean that you are not worthy of punishing yourself or of being punished? (+)*

Q. *Must you punish yourself in order to be okay? (+)*

Q. *Are you controlled by your mother? (+)*

Q. *Must you be controlled by her? (+)*

Q. *If you clean house, do you break her control? (+)*

Q. *Is that wrong? (+)*

Q. *Does a cluttered house keep you from attracting men?* (+)

Q. *Does a dirty house keep you safe from men?* (+)

Q. *Would a clean house blow your safety?* (+)

Q. *If you cleaned house, would you become a harlot?* (+)

Ella was not in control of her life; her discordant programs were. Since Ella has worked with Spiritual Response Therapy, many people have remarked that they can see positive changes in her. However, this is one client who needs ongoing counseling to help her put her life in order and keep it there.

Case study #2: Unworthy of greater self-esteem

Leah had discordant energy on her gentleman friend and the sole reason was conflict. Their relationship had never been a smooth one and another woman was involved which made it an on-again/off-again relationship. Leah could not understand why she had anything to do with Bill at all.

Q. *Do you and Bill belong together?* (+)

Q. *Is there something to be learned from your being together?* (+)

Q. *Does he help you build greater self-esteem?* (+)

Q. *Is that your purpose together?* (+)

Q. *When that purpose is fulfilled, can you release him?* (+)

Q. *Are you threatened by his desire to help you build greater self-esteem?* (+)

Q. *Do you want to build greater self-esteem?* (+)

Q. *Are you unworthy of greater self-esteem?* (+)

Leah had several reasons to feel unworthy of greater self-esteem. She had been a drug addict, alcoholic, and prostitute. She was completely estranged from her family and was experiencing considerable difficulty in her personal relationships as well as on her job. Nothing seemed to be working for her. When she came for counseling, she was desperate.

Q. *Do you want to love Bill but cannot because of the discordant factors we have found?* (+)

Q. *Is there any other reason?* (+)

Q. *Is the conflict that Bill is too pure for you?* (+)

Q. *Is the conflict involved with the other woman?* (+)

Q. *Is there a karmic tie involved?* (+)

Q. *When was the tie established?* (past lives)

Q. *Was there a triangle involved then as there is now?* (+)

Q. *Was rejection involved?* (+)

Q. *Did the other woman reject Bill?* (+)

Q. *Did Bill turn to you after his rejection?* (+)

Q. *Is that the conflict now? You hope the other woman will reject Bill and you will get him again?* (+)

Q. *Is there any other reason for the conflict?* (-)

Leah's self-esteem was so low that she had great difficulty repeating the releasing statements. Getting her to say them was like pulling deeply driven nails out of a block of wood with only your fingernails. I could not give her a releasing statement† like: "I release my belief, perception and judgment that Bill is too pure for me." She would shudder all over, clench her fists, and burst into tears. The releasing statements had to be fed to her a few words at a time which she was able to repeat: "I release...my belief...perception...and judgment...that Bill...is too pure...for me." Even then, Leah had to be coaxed into making the statements. Often the simple phrases had to be repeated several times before she could speak them.

Before Leah came to me she had spent some fifty hours in counseling, and was suffering from anxiety and depression. There was little that was going right in her life and she was extremely confused regarding the purpose of her own life and the value of staying around. Our work together involved six, two hour sessions. Several weeks after we had completed our meetings, I saw Leah at church. I asked her how she was doing. She was very excited and

---

†Since High Self can clear all programs, releasing statements are not necessary, but they can be of great benefit in certain situations, as explained in Chapter 3.

informed me that every facet of her life had changed for the better. Her relationship with her mother, which had always been bitter, had improved tremendously and they were communicating and enjoying each other's company. Leah was now getting along very well with her employer. People at work who had previously insulted her and put her down, were coming to her, apologizing, and asking to be friends again. She was at peace for the first time in her life and was looking forward to each day with a joyful anticipation of good things happening.

Case study #3: Conflict program causing ill health

Iris had a problem with her health with one reason—a program of conflict. She was a gifted, intuitive person. As we worked together, she had many insights that helped pinpoint the problem.

Q. *Do you want to be healthy? (+)*

Q. *Are you supposed to have all wisdom? (+)*

Q. *Are you a spiritual being? (+)*

Q. *Do you feel worthy of expressing God-life and wisdom? (-)*

Q. *Must you punish yourself for not being worthy? (+)*

Q. *Have you done a lot of things to merit punishment? (+)*

Q. *Must you keep from reflecting any human traits? (+)*

Q. *Are your human emotions a block to your spiritual development? (+)*

Q. *Can you have emotions and be spiritual? (-)*

Q. *Are you punishing yourself by having health challenges? (+)*

Q. *So the conflict is that you would like to be free from health challenges, but cannot be free because you must punish yourself by being sick? (+)*

Q. *Because you are failing to be spiritual, all wise, and free from human emotions? (+)*

Q. *Is it all right to let go of these discordant programs now? (+)*

Next we worked on Iris' relationship with a gentleman friend. The discordant energy was ninety percent and there were six reasons. Conflict ran through all of the reasons, even the reason of eight past lives. We only had to look at three past lives in order to clear the discordant energy. Iris and her friend were homosexuals in at least one past life. Because he is gay in this life, she could neither love him completely nor be at peace in their present relationship.

During another past life, they were both priests and involved in a power struggle concerning the number of gods. She believed in many gods and he believed in one. There was even physical conflict between them. Because she could not convert him in the past life, she felt she could not love him completely now.

In a third past life, they were both spiritual teachers on Atlantis and involved in a power struggle over whose beliefs were correct. Both used mind energy to control and manipulate resulting in a stand-off with neither being able to convert the other. Iris felt very guilty now because she had failed then and was punishing herself by being in conflict. Although she had physically saved his life during the Atlantean time, she could not convert him to her beliefs and thus save his soul. She felt guilty because she was unable to explain her beliefs clearly enough to cause his conversion.

Iris was in conflict in her relationship with him in this life because, again, she could not convince him that her way of life was correct and that his was wrong.

Q. *Are you in conflict because he won't let you convert him? (+)*

Q. *Because his emotions are out of control? (+)*

Q. *Because you resent placating him—giving in to him? (+)*

Q. *Because he is unpredictable and emotionally dishonest? (+)*

Q. *Any other reason for the discordant energy? (-)*

CHAPTER 15

Self-Punishment

ཀྵ ལ

Have you ever noticed that when you do something you consider wrong, there is a sense of guilt and a resulting desire to punish yourself. The guilt and self-punishment may be brought into this life as a result of things you have done or not done in past lives. As if that is not enough, you are usually taught to feel guilty in this life at a very early age. So its no wonder that every person with whom I have worked has been, at least to some degree, caught up in self-punishment. The reasons are myriad. The slightest perceived infraction in thought, feeling, or action can trigger a response of self-punishment.

The reasons for feeling guilty and the need to punish yourself are usually very intertwined, convoluted and extremely controlling. Once self-punishment programs are established, they take over and cause difficulties that may destroy every opportunity to experience the good things of life. Peace, relationships, prosperity, health, love, and even life—all are sacrificed on the altar of guilt and self-punishment.

Strangely, there is often a catch twenty-two aspect to self-punishment. You punish yourself by exhibiting the exact behavior you are punishing yourself for expressing, such as: by eating too much to punish yourself for eating too much. Or, you might punish yourself for being unworthy by acting in such a way as to make yourself unworthy. Thus, the program perpetuates itself in a constant downward spiral.

Suicide

The need and desire to punish the self can be so deep seated that suicide, extreme injury,

terminal illness, or even death by accident is the result. Accidental death or terminal illness is simply another way (through a subconscious decision) of committing suicide and may be more acceptable to the person than using a deliberate, conscious means of leaving the body.

Many people have committed suicide in former lives and may have a suicide program trying to manifest itself in this life. These people may not have succeeded in driving the life out of their body or may not even have attempted to do so, but to a greater or lesser degree, they have succeeded in slaying their good. There seems to be a destructive tendency or self-limiting, self-punishing tendency in the way they are living their life. Nothing good seems to come to them and if it does they will find some way to destroy it. Once the suicide program is uncovered and released, things always change for the better.

Forgiveness

Guilt that was established in a former life must be met and worked through in subsequent lives. The best time to deal with guilt, old or new, is in the present life through forgiveness of self and others, "Agree with (forgive) thine adversary quickly, whiles thou art in the way with him; lest at any time the adversary deliver thee to the judge, and the judge deliver thee to the officer, and thou be cast into prison" (Matthew 5:25). Once the discordant energy is set up, it must be dealt with at some time in some place. Until it is dealt with, you are in prison—the prison of your own discordant energies.

Once you meet and overcome the discordant programming, you are free of the judgments made. Jesus said, "Judge not, and ye shall not be judged: condemn not, and ye shall not be condemned: forgive and ye shall be forgiven" (Luke, 6:37). Releasing the belief that the hurtful situation ever happened in the first place is the most powerful form of forgiveness available to man today. Pain and taking offense are not of God. There is only love, therefore there can be no offense. Regardless of the situation, you have the power and ability to know the truth, and thus, to choose to forgive rather than to take offense. "Then came Peter to him, and said, 'Lord, how often shall my brother sin against me, and I forgive him? Till seven times seven?' Jesus saith unto him, 'I say not unto thee, until seven times: but, until seventy times seven.' " (Matthew, 18:21-22). The seventy times seven simply means as many times as is necessary to release the discordant energy.

With the releasing statements† used in Spiritual Response Therapy it usually only takes once. Also, as soon as there is a conscious awareness of a discordant energy creeping in, it can be immediately slain, by using releasing statements, before it gains a foothold in the subconscious mind.

As you will see from the examples given later in this chapter, there is often nothing rational about self-punishment.

Technique

To research self-punishment programs, use the standard technique as explained in Chapter 7. Self-punishment programs can be irrational or seem convoluted. Refer to the case studies at the end of this chapter to get a sense of how to ask questions to discover the reasons for self-punishment.

Oftentimes while researching self-punishment programs, a "no" response will be received when asking if there are programs to research or if the programs can be cleared. If you encounter this, simply ask High Self to administer a "spiritual kick." This opens the door, giving you access to the person's programs and allows High Self to clear them. Sometimes it takes a

lot of clearing work to clear a person's self-punishment programs.

Technique to Clear Basic Life Theme of Self-Punishment

While working with a discordant energy in your life, it may become very apparent that a desire for self-punishment or some self-restrictive theme is involved. It is easy to end up in the prison of your own discordant programs and remain there for several lifetimes. Many people have a basic program of self-punishment that is set up as a part of the total expression for this life. Should you run into a lot of self-punishment while clearing your programs or someone else's programs, check to see if it is a basic life theme. (For more information on life themes, see my book, *Soul Re-Creation, Developing your Cosmic Potential* which presents advanced techniques of Spiritual Response Therapy.)

Q. Is there a life theme of self-punishment? (+)

Q. To what percent is this theme controlling the current life?

Here is a meditation technique I use to help clear a basic life theme of self-punishment. I call this process "cleaning the files." (To use this meditation for yourself, record it on an audio tape and play it back).

Sit in a comfortable chair. Take a deep breath and relax. Imagine yourself in a beautiful garden. There are paths winding through beautiful green lawns, and many beautiful flower beds line the paths. There are flowering trees and the air is filled with the fragrance of their perfume. Bees are busy gathering nectar and the air is filled with exquisite butterflies of every color. The sweet song of birds is all around you and you are at peace. Follow the path as it curves gracefully through the garden. Enjoy the peace, beauty, and tranquility of this magical place. Rounding a curve in the path, you see before you a beautiful temple made of crystal white marble and you know it is your private sanctuary away from the cares and toils of the world.

There are ten steps leading up to the sanctuary. Take the steps slowly, one-by-one, as I count. With each step you will ascend into a higher

---

†Since High Self can clear all programs, releasing statements are not necessary, but they can be of great benefit in certain situations, as explained in Chapter 3.

state of consciousness. One. You are rising from an earthbound state into a spiritual state. Two. You are becoming deeply relaxed and drifting deeper into this state. Three. Going deeper. Four. Deeper still. Five. You are very relaxed and centered within. Six...seven...eight...you are approaching the zenith of a spiritual experience. Nine...ten. You are now deep within—at the door of the temple.

To the right of the door is a rack. Take off your shoes and place them in the rack, for you stand on holy ground. On top of the rack are white gowns—put one on. As you approach the door, it slides silently open. When you are inside, it slides closed behind you. There is no visible source of light but the room is illumined by a soft glow that seems to fill the very air. Move to the left wall. There is a file cabinet built into the wall. It may consist of only one drawer or many. To one side of the file there is a door about two feet wide and three feet high. Near the top of the door there is a handle. This door opens like a laundry chute directly into the furnace of everlasting fire.

There is a nameplate on the file cabinet that reads: Self-punishment. Open the file drawer. Inside are hanging files. Some of them may have material in them. These are all of your records of self-punishment. Take them out and throw them into the furnace. If the file fills up again, empty it again. Make certain all of the files are gone. Check the cabinet for papers in the bottom of the file that may have fallen out of the folders. There may even be a book in which you have recorded all of the hurts connected to self-punishment. Throw it into the furnace. When the file is completely empty, move back toward the entrance.

There is a chair built just for you. Sit down and relax. In front of you is a movie screen. It may come down from the ceiling or it may stand on legs. See on the screen a figure of yourself the way you are right now with all of your faults and imperfections. Let's call it the old you. Reach up, and with your left hand, move the figure off the screen to the left until it disappears. With your right hand, reach up and move a new light-filled-being onto the screen from the right. This is the new you, free and filled with spirit. "Ye are the light of the world, let your light shine" (Matthew 5:14).

In front of you is a table with a candle on it. What color is the candle? As you breathe in, see a ball of light at the crown of your head. As you breathe out, see it flow down into your body dissolving all darkness and limitation. It is like breathing in through the top of your head and breathing out through your fingers and toes. Continue this breathing until your whole body is filled with light. Now gather the light at your heart center. Send the light out in a beam to touch the candle before you on the table. It immediately springs into flame. Look deeply into the flame—hold your attention there. A tiny figure dressed in white appears at the center of the flame. It steps out of the flame and begins to grow until it is life-size. There is a powerful sense of peace and love that emanates from this figure. This is your High Self which moves toward you and embraces you. Hear it say, "I have loved you with an everlasting love. I will never leave you nor forsake you. I am with you always, even unto the end of the world." Then the High Self merges with you and you are one. You may stay in your meditation room with your High Self as long as you wish. Know that from now on, wherever you go, your High Self is with you.

Now it is time to leave the temple. As you move toward the door, it slides silently open before you and closes behind you. Take off the garment and place it on the rack. Put on your shoes. Descend the stairs and make your way back through the garden. There has been a shower while you were in the temple and everything is fresh and bright. The birds' singing is more intense and the butterflies and flowers are even more brilliant than before. Everything is enhanced and you are filled with joy for you know that God is with you and you are blessed.

As you walk slowly through the garden enjoying the fresh beauty, you see a beautiful rainbow with its foot in the path before you. Unlike all the rainbows you've seen before, it does not recede before you as you approach. Walk up to the rainbow and enter into it. You are one with the rich promise of God. You are free!

This method of cleaning out the subconscious files is effective for any program that is deep seated and keeps recurring while working to clear your discordant programs. The program may be one of anger, fear, hate, low self-esteem, etc.

Case study #1: Discordant energy on mother
Excess weight
Low self-esteem

Iris was a business woman with a lot of knowledge and ability. Yet, with all of her hard work she seemed unable to eke out more than marginal existence. Her sales were always just enough to take care of bills with nothing left over to enjoy the good things of life. With intense feelings of guilt, Iris described her mother as highly emotional, overworked, and a wonderful cook. Iris identified with the highly emotional and overworked traits. Her guilt was increased because she believed she should be a good cook like her mother but was not. She accepted the benefit of guilt as a means of pleasing her mother and to prove she loved her mother. Also, Iris was in conflict because she wanted to be like her mother but could not because she did not want to be emotional. Here are her self-punishment programs related to discordant programs on her mother:

Q. *Are you punishing yourself by being highly emotional? (+)*

Q. *Are you punishing yourself by being overworked? (+)*

Q. *Is there any other reason of self-punishment? (+)*

Additionally, she held these self-punishment programs:

Q. *Are you punishing yourself by being overweight? (+)*

Q. *By being celibate? (+)*

Q. *Any other reason? (-)*

She also had a self-punishment program on a friend who was slim and trim. Weight also entered into this punishment.

Q. *Are you punishing yourself because she is slim and you are not? (+)*

Q. *Because you are a failure at losing weight? (+)*

Q. *Because you are more spiritual than she is? (+)*

Q. *Any other reason? (-)*

Because of her programs of low self-esteem, Iris was very good at creating these seemingly

extraneous reasons for self-punishment. Unfortunately, the self-punishment was only causing her self-esteem to decrease. Self-punishment never serves any constructive purpose.

Q. *Are you punishing yourself because you are imperfect? (+)*

Q. *Because you are human? (+)*

Q. *Because you are lazy? (+)*

Q. *Are you fat so you can punish yourself? (+)*

Q. *Are you fat so you can be perfect? (+)*

Q. *Are you fat so you can be protected from burning? (+) (This referred to a former life wherein she was burned as a witch.)*

Q. *Are you punishing yourself by being single? (+)*

Q. *Must you be single and support yourself? (+)*

Q. *So you can prove you are capable? (+)*

Q. *Haven't you already proven that? (-) (Iris is a very capable person who has operated her own business successfully for many years.)*

Q. *Are you not successful and supporting yourself now? (-)*

Q. *Is there any other reason for self-punishment? (-)*

Case study #2: Low self-esteem

Judy identified with her mother, father, aunt, brother, and psychiatrist all of whom, in her opinion, had low self-esteem. Judy suffered from low self-esteem and had spent countless hours counseling with a person with the same problem according to her subconscious record.

Much of Judy's problem with self-esteem was caused by former lives and even led to attempted suicide in this life. When I met her, she had withdrawn from society and was fearful of going out into the world to obtain gainful employment. Again, her fear of going out into public was involved with a former life. She had been a great religious leader and had many followers. Because of what she perceived as her personal failure as a religious leader, she had caused the death of many of her followers and lost her own life as well.

Q. *Are you punishing yourself because you failed your people in that former life? (+)*

Q. Do you have low self-esteem so you can restrict your expression of life now as self-punishment? (+)

Q. Are you punishing yourself for being born? (+)

Q. Should you have changed your mind and not been born? (+)

Q. Did you cause your mother pain at birth? (+)

Q. Are you punishing yourself for causing her pain? (+)

Another of Judy's self-punishment programs was rooted in a past life in another dimension in which she had caused injury and death through her misapplication of computers. She had a natural talent for working with computers in her present life but was fearful of doing so because she might again cause injury or even death. She was punishing herself now by having low self-esteem. Because of her past life training, she was highly qualified for work with computers, but prohibited from using these talents because of low self-esteem.

Several months after we cleared Judy, I heard she had found employment in the computer industry and her employer was so pleased with her abilities that he gave her a raise almost immediately. Her self-esteem had skyrocketed and she is relaxed and enjoying life for the first time in many years. She no longer has a desire to commit suicide or a fear that she might try to do so again. Judy feels good about herself and her new life reflects her altered subconscious programs.

Case study #3: Buffer between parents
Lack of spiritual accomplishment

Dawn seemed completely poised and centered when she came to see me. She earned her livelihood as a counselor and was quite successful. However, she felt limited and desired to find out why. One of the first things we found was that Dawn had a program of self-punishment regarding her parent's relationship. She saw herself as a buffer between them. Her job was to divert their attention from each other so they would not fight or argue. She stopped their problems by coming between them. Her major self-punishment program began when she went into puberty.

Q. Was puberty a threat to your parent's relationship? (+)

Q. You could no longer be a buffer? (+)

Q. Did your growing up put your parent's relationship more out of control? (+)

Q. Were you failing in your responsibility? (+)

Q. Are you punishing yourself for that? (+)

Q. Any other reason to punish yourself? (-)

Dawn held discordant energy on herself and had another program of self-punishment that involved four past lives. In one life she was a ruler with a religious bent. She had turned away from God and thus failed her people. In the second life she broke away from the Catholic Church to follow Martin Luther. The third life found her as the wife of a great religious teacher in India. She felt as if she had failed to present his teachings in a meaningful way. In the fourth life, Dawn was a nun. She had betrayed the love of a sister nun and had harmed her by driving her crazy. Her self-punishment programs centered around her seeming lack of spiritual accomplishment in this life. Although she was an excellent healer and psychic, she was putting a lot of guilt on herself for not being more spiritual and doing more to reveal her spiritual nature.

Q. Are you failing to express your spiritual nature? (+)

Q. Are you punishing yourself for failing to fulfill your divine potential? (+)

Q. For not listening to your guidance? (+)

Q. For not being perfect? (+)

Q. For not taking enough time alone with your inner self? (+)

Q. For failing to fulfill your parent's plan for your life? (+)

Q. For still being married to Ted? (+)

Q. Is he keeping you from being spiritual? (+)

Q. For the abortion you had? (+) (Consciously, she felt okay about the abortion but her subconscious was troubled.)

Q. Did the abortion cause you to be less spiritual? (+)

Q. Are you punishing yourself for being in the world? (+)

Q. Do you have a basic program that you are not okay and need to punish yourself? (+)

Q. Are you punishing yourself because you are not worthy of having your life the way you want it? (+)

These programs and others were cleared and her life has taken on new meaning and direction. Her meditations have deepened and her healing abilities have been enhanced. She has a lot of ability and her sole desire is to serve others which she is now doing more fully than before.

Case study #4:   Difficulty communicating

Ann's self-punishment programs were many and involved. She experienced a lot of trauma in her occupation as a school teacher because she felt that she did a very poor job of communicating with her students. Ann's lack of communication was a form of self-limitation and self-punishment. She punished herself for everything imaginable.

Q. Are you punishing yourself for not suffering enough? (+)

Q. Are you more spiritual when you punish yourself? (+)

Q. Because you were not a boy like your father wanted? (+)

Q. Because you failed to stop your father's drinking? (+)

Q. Are you his savior? (-)

Q. Did you fail to save him? (+)

Q. Because you are responsible for your aunt's alcoholism? (+)

Q. Did you fail in your responsibility to keep her quiet and bring peace? (+)

Q. Are you punishing yourself by not being good enough to communicate with others? (+)

Q. Did you talk too much in the past? (+)

Q. Are you punishing yourself for being a sinner? (+)

Q. Are you guilty of being imperfect? (+)

Since clearing, life has greatly expanded for Ann. Communication has not only improved with her students but with everyone else in her life. She is more at peace and finding the renewed relationship with her former mate more peaceful and rewarding.

Case study #5:   Use of foul language

Ben had only one reason for the discordant energy on Herbert, his grandfather, and it was self-punishment.

Q. Is the self-punishment because of guilt? (+)

Q. When was the guilt established? (present life, age two)

Q. Did you do something to your grandfather? (-)

Q. Did you do something to your grandmother? (+)

Q. Was it something you said to her? (+)

Q. Did you use foul language? (+)

Q. Did you call her a name? (+)

Q. Anything else we need to know on this self-punishment? (-)

Q. Any other reason for discordant energy on your grandfather? (+)

Q. What is the area? (Using the chart and a pendulum, we found it to be experience/ trauma.)

Q. Was it because your grandfather punished you for using foul language? (+)

Q. Were you angry at your grandfather? (+)

Q. Any other reason for the discordant energy on him? (-)

Ben's discordant programs were very expansive, deeply imbedded, and strongly reinforced. Nearly a year has passed since I last worked with him. His almost constant depression has been eliminated so that he only occasionally finds himself in a confused state of mind. However, there is still much for Ben to do before we can say, "Hooray! Praise God, Ben is free."

Case study #6:   Relationship with mother

May was caught up in a lot of emotional energy regarding her mother's illness and subsequent death. Her mother was often harsh and critical of May and May did not feel good about her relationship with her mother. She was experiencing a lot of emotional pain and a strong sense of guilt since her mother's death and wanted to clear up that energy. She had ninety-five percent discordant energy on her mother with twelve reasons. May identified her mother as discordant, harping, critical, stingy, jealous, non-supportive, and having low self-esteem. Her mother had a seizure when May was twenty-five and May felt that her mother had it coming. Her mother even told May that she, May, almost got her way when she wished her mother would die. Here are the reasons for self-punishment:

Q. *Were you guilty for not being there when your mother died? (+)*

Q. *Because of your statement that you wished she would die? (+)*

Q. *Because you failed to give your mother proper care? (+)*

Q. *Any other reason of self-punishment? (+)*

Q. *More than one? (-)*

Q. *What is the area? (one past life)*

Q. *Was the relationship the same as now? (+)*

Her mother had been cruel and abused May mentally and emotionally in that life. Even though her mother was ill, May allowed her to go out in a snowstorm and she died. Although it was an accidental death, May felt that she had failed to give her mother proper attention and she had been cruel toward her mother. The energy has at last been released and there need be no further recurrence of it in a future life.

May had ninety-five percent discordant energy on her grandmother. As with her mother, it was mixed up in identification, imprint, conflict, and past lives. Again, she felt as if she had failed to care for her grandmother properly and had caused her death. She needed to punish herself to expiate her guilt.

CHAPTER 16

Organ Language
ဢ ၽ

There are two types of organ language: body comparison and body statements. Organ language can be established for anyone any time throughout life.

With body comparison, you hold discordant energy on yourself and on the person you are compared to physically, mentally or emotionally.

"That makes me sick to my stomach." "He gives me a pain in the neck." "That's a headache to me." Body statements such as these are perfect examples of organ language. When frequently repeated, these statements and others like them cause discordant energy to be held on yourself or someone else. They also can cause physical difficulties to be experienced in the body. The actual physical condition repeatedly spoken about may develop. Chronic headaches, colds, allergies (especially hay fever), pains, throat difficulties, stomach pains, etc., seem to rise from organ language.

Some of the common statements we hear every day are, on the surface, seemingly harmless yet there is a great possibility of the words manifesting in a very destructive way. Here are a few common statements that we would do well to drop from our language. "That just slays me." "That just burns me up." "That gives me a pain in the neck." There are a host of such statements. Some of them seem laughable, but they are not.

Although organ language is not encountered as frequently as the other programs, it still carries discordant energy and must be researched and released. Should any discordant energy be left regarding a person's programs, it tends to

rebuild and cause further problems. Only when you know the truth of your inner programs, can they be released and new, positive ones established to bring good results.

Technique

To research organ language programs, use the standard technique as explained in Chapter 7.

When a client requests a clearing, they usually discuss the people and energies involved in their life and this helps the counselor be aware of possible problem areas. When there does not seem to be obvious answers to a situation, simply ask the client what they consciously think or what they are feeling about the situation. This often gives clues to additional questions to ask.

More clues can be found in the other types of programs. I found organ language to be tricky until I learned to look for clues among the other programs.

Case study #1: Sexual fantasies

Jack, mentioned in the chapter on experience/trauma, spent a lot of his time in sexual fantasies which caused him pain. There were eight reasons for the pain and one of them was organ language.

Q. *Will you be using your mind in the wrong way? (+)*

Q. *Will you be using your body in the wrong way? (+)*

These answers seem simplistic, as they usually do. However, they are not always easy to find.

Case study #2:   Excess weight
Self-punishment

Ella, mentioned in several previous chapters, had discordant energy on her brother caused by organ language. After a lot of questions that elicited "no" answers, we found that he had said she was ugly. When we worked on the discordant energy she held on herself, we again found organ language.

Q. *Does it have to do with your being over-weight? (+)*

Q. *Can you be overweight and still love your-self? (-)*

Q. *The only way you can love yourself is to be slim? (+)*

Q. *Any other reason of organ language? (-)*

Ella had an extremely strong program of self-punishment involved with organ language.

Q. *Is the organ language that you are fat and sick? (+)*

Q. *Are you fat and sick so you can punish yourself? (+)*

Q. *Must you be fat and sick so you can punish yourself? (+)*

Q. *Must you punish yourself? (+)*

Case study #3:   Excess weight

Iris, mentioned in several preceding chapters, had a lot of programs in regard to her weight. She was a prolific reader and although she wanted to cut down on the amount of reading she just could not seem to do so. One of the seven reasons was organ language. The infor-mation does not always appear logical, but this is what we found:

Q. *Did you write erotic literature in Egypt? (+)*

Q. *Did you have it carved in stone? (+)*

Q. *Does your body have to be large so you can carry all of the knowledge you have learned? (+)*

Q. *Does carrying all of this knowledge exhaust you? (+)*

Q. *Do vibrations (words) on paper exhaust you? (+)*

Q. *Does carrying all this knowledge make your body tired? (+)*

There was a lot of guilt involved with the past life in Egypt and the writings she caused to be carved in stone. Her large physical organ (body) was a form of self-punishment. It is amazing how energy can be carried over from one lifetime to another. Seldom have I worked with a client without finding past lives involved with the current life problems.

Iris also had a fear of becoming a sex object. The program was: "if she were thin she would become a sex object," hence her large physical body. In addition, she was afraid that if she were slim, she could not say "no" to men or food.

Case study #4:   Body comparison
Love for grandmother

This is a case of body comparison. Tim had a problem with excess weight. His organ lan-guage on his father was that he was too large and that made Tim fat also.

Concurrently, he had seven reasons for being heavy and overweight and one of the reasons was an organ language program.

Q. *Is this a statement you made about your-self? (+)*

Q. *Did you tell yourself you were fat and always would be? (+)*

Q. *Did you tell yourself you must be fat to prove you love your grandmother? (+)*

Q. *Any other reason of organ language? (-)*

Many of the questions I ask, such as the one about the grandmother, are based on the conscious observations of the client.

Case study #5:   Discordant energy on God

Tina had so many mental, emotional, and physical ailments it was difficult to determine what was the major cause of her problems. She had extremely low self-esteem and held a lot of discordant energy on herself and on God. There were six reasons to hold discordant energy on God, with one reason being an organ language program.

Q. *Is it God's fault you are heavy? (+)*

Q. *Does He want you to be heavy? (+)*

Q. *Is your arthritis God's will? (+)*

Q. *Is the blood disorder God's will? (+)*

Q. *Are the gout and sour stomach His will? (+)*

Q. *Do you have hepatitis? (+)*

Q. *Do you have a liver problem? (+)*

Q. *Is all disease God's will?* (+)

Q. *Any other reason of organ language to hold discordant energy on God?* (+)

Q. *Is it God's fault that man abuses the animals?* (+)

Q. *Any other reason?* (-)

Case study #6:   Discordant energy on daughter

Ernestine had a reason of organ language to hold discordant energy on her daughter.

Q. *Because you are shorter than your daughter?* (+)

Q. *Because she uses her body in a threatening way?* (+)

Case study #7:   Discordant energy on father

Alice had discordant energy on her father due to organ language programs caused because her father sexually, mentally, emotionally, and physically abused her in every conceivable way.

Case study #8:   Unworthy of self-love

Researching the discordant energy Leah (mentioned in the chapter on conflict) held on herself led to organ language programs as well as identification, imprint, and conflict programs. Her life style of being sexually promiscuous, involved in the drug scene, deceitful, a liar, and a cheater made her subconscious conclude she was completely unworthy of self-love. Using this information as clues, we found the organ language.

Q. *Does it have to do with your sexuality?* (+)

Q. *Is your body unclean?* (-)

Q. *Have you used your body in the wrong way?* (+)

Q. *Wrong involvement with drugs and sex?* (+)

Q. *Wrong diet and lack of exercise?* (+)

Q. *Are you using all of this to punish yourself?* (+)

At the same time, Leah had an experience/trauma program that went back to a painful birth in which she was emotionally injured because her mother did not want her to be born. She had a subconscious death wish and the drug and prostitution was a way of destroying herself a little bit at a time. She told herself that life was not worth living and was punishing herself for being here at all. She felt she should have changed her mind and not

been born. She was punishing herself for having failed to live to her higher life potential. She had a strong desire to punish and limit herself on the one hand, and on the other hand she was punishing herself for being limited.

Case study #9:   Excess weight

Mary Jane had organ language on her parents. Her father said she was overweight. Also, neither of her parents were able, because of their own early programming, to show any expression of love and affection toward her. They simply were not using their bodies in a meaningful and loving way.

Case study #10: Physical and emotional pain

Katie, whom I mentioned in previous chapters, also had an organ language program involved with her fear of again taking up her work as a court reporter.

Q. *Does being a court reporter cause you physical pain?* (+)

Q. *Does working as a court reporter cause you emotional pain?* (+)

Q. *Any other reason of organ language?* (-)

Katie had experienced intense physical and emotional pain all her life. The court reporter job became the straw that was simply too much to carry. Through Spiritual Response Therapy she once again found meaning and purpose in her life and is working at her old profession and loving it. When I saw her recently, I asked her how she was doing. "Terrific!!" she said.

Case study #11: Headaches and sinus problems

Headaches often have their beginnings in organ language. Fred, mentioned in the chapter on experience/trauma, used a double imprint and organ language to generate headaches. This program resulted from his relationship with his father.

Q. *Did your father say you had a big head?* (+)

Q. *Did he say it was full of stuff you should not have?* (+)

Q. *Is that a reason for having sinus problems?* (+)

Q. *Did he say you gave him a headache?* (+)

Q. *Are you punishing yourself for being a headache to him?* (+)

Q.   *Are you punishing yourself by having headaches?* *(+)*

Q.   *Do you have sinus problems so you can have headaches?* *(+)*

Q.   *Is the sinus a result of having too much in your head to handle?* *(+)*

Q.   *Is too much in your head to handle causing you headaches?* *(+)*

There were also a couple of traumatic experiences causing the headaches covered in the chapter on experience/trauma. Six months after Fred concluded his work with Spiritual Response Therapy, he came back for a follow up session. The headaches had been greatly reduced, but he was still having headaches. There were some additional reasons of self-punishment that were found and released.

CHAPTER 17

Past Lives

✆ ◌

The energies you have established in past lives may have a tremendous effect on your current life. Discordant energies you set up, regardless of when they were established, must be dissolved at some point in time if you would be completely free.

There is a law in the universe that is basic to all of life. It is the law of giving and receiving. Jesus said, "Judge not, that ye be not judged. For with what judgment ye judge, ye shall be judged: and with what measure ye mete, it shall be measured to you again" (Matthew, 7:1-2). The ultimate in giving and receiving is not material goods, but the essence of your mind and heart—or mental and emotional energy. The material goods you give, are simply the outer expression of your thoughts and feelings which become the things of the world. Giving the positive energy of mind and heart (these are the things that are real and lasting and have the greatest meaning) returns to you results that are positive and constructive. Sending out discordant energy draws a discordant return.

The Old Testament puts it very succinctly, "An eye for an eye" (Exodus, 21:24). You receive a return on the mental and emotional energy you emit—so it benefits you to send only what you want returned, not what you do not want returned. The energy you sow in one life may be reaped in another, unless something is done to change it or to dissolve it. If the energy is positive and loving, that is well for both the sender and the receiver.

Desire To Commit Suicide

I have worked with a lot of people in Spiritual Response Therapy who have either had a desire to commit physical suicide, or who have been self-destructive in every facet of their life. In each instance, there have been past lives involved where the person has committed suicide. Seldom does the root cause of a desire to commit suicide have its sole inception in this life, although it can be set up because of current pressures of living.

There are many types of programs which can contribute to a desire to commit suicide. If you have a client for whom this is an issue, refer to the suicide entry in the Index for a list of all references to suicide. You may also wish to read all of the case studies in which suicide is an issue. These are listed in the Index and in the Index of Case Studies at the back of this book.

Technique

To research past life programs, use the standard technique as explained in Chapter 7.

Many of the people I counsel do not believe in past lives. Yet, seldom have I worked with any client without past lives being the source of some of the current life problems they are encountering. Not wishing to convince someone against their will that they have lived before, I completely research the first eight programs listed on Chart 2 in an attempt to find the reasons for a problem.

Q. Is it an inheritance program?

If I receive a "yes" response, I research the program(s) in the usual manner. If I receive a "no" response, I ask if it is the next type of program.

Q. Is it an identification program?

If after exhausting the first eight programs, there is still a reason for the problem, I simply hand the chart to the client and ask them to use the pendulum to find the reason. They are quite amazed to see the pendulum swing toward "past lives" as the reason for a current problem. I always verify the movement by asking if it is a reason of past lives. Case study #1 illustrates this circumstance.

Case study #1:   Arguing on school grounds

Carl, an eleven year old boy, and his mother came to see me because he was having problems at school. There was no difficulty in the classroom with his teachers or with other students. But, when he was outside of the classroom, he was constantly in arguments. These arguments were becoming such a problem that the school officials were considering suspending Carl.

The process of release counseling was explained to Carl and the movements of the pendulum were quickly established and confirmed.

Q. *Are you constantly arguing on the school grounds? (+)*

Q. *Are there two or more reasons for the arguments? (-)*

Q. *Is there only one reason? (+)*

Q. *Is it an inheritance program? (-)*

Q. *Is it an identification program? (-)*

Q. *Is it an imprint program? (-)*

Q. *Is it an experience/trauma program? (-)*

I continued in this manner until I had eliminated the first eight programs listed on Chart 2 (as explained in the Technique section above). I was certain that Carl did not believe in past lives and was concerned what his reaction would be when asked if that was the reason—would he consciously block a response? However, when I asked him if it was a reason of past lives, the pendulum was immediately moved in a "yes" direction. Considering that he was always into debates on the school grounds led me to ask the following question.

Q. *Were you a great orator or debater in a previous life? (+)*

Q. *Is that why you are always arguing on the school grounds? (+)*

Q. *Any other reason for the arguments? (-)*

I did not want to remove the possibility that he could use the talent he had developed in the past life for speaking or debating in this life, but I did want to clear him of the need to debate on the school grounds. I had him make these releasing statements:[†]

> *"I release my belief, perception and judgment that because I was a great speaker or debater in a previous life I must argue on the school grounds now. I release all need or desire to argue on the school grounds now. I release all need and desire to believe anything but I am free from arguing on the school grounds now. However, I may use my talents as an orator, as I grow up, to become a great speaker in my chosen profession."*

It had taken only about thirty minutes to set up the system with Carl, find all of the necessary information, clear the program and put in the new program. When Carl came in one week later, I asked him how many times he had been in arguments on the school grounds. He informed me that he had not had any arguments at all—not even one. Then he went on to say that he believed the reason he had been arguing was because he always argued with his little sister at home. I handed him the pendulum.

Q. *Was it because you always argue with your little sister at home? (-)*

Q. *Was it because of past lives? (+)*

When he got home, he had a long talk with his grandmother about the meaning of life, what happens when you die and about reincarnation. The change in Carl was dramatic. During the rest of the school term, he had no further trouble with arguments on the school grounds.

Case study #2:   Past life suicide

The case of Tony was presented in the chapter on imprints. The third time that Tony came in to see me he looked very down. I asked him how things were going. He informed me that he was very frightened. He had thought about suicide from time to time over the years but

---

[†]If you ask High Self to clear the program and replace it with good, you do not need to have any similar concerns. They will make sure that only the discordant situations are cleared and the good remain.

not seriously. Now thoughts of suicide were very strong and he had, since our last session, been thinking of ways to commit suicide. I immediately began the questioning process to find out what was going on.

Q. *Do you have a desire to commit suicide? (+)*

Q. *What is the program? (Identification, Chart 2)*

We then proceeded to eliminate people with whom he might be identifying. We kept getting "no" responses. Out of desperation, I asked him if he was identifying with himself.

Q. *Are you identifying with yourself? (+)*

Q. *Is this a current life identification? (-)*

Q. *Are you identifying with yourself from a past life? (+)*

Q. *Did you commit suicide in a former life? (+)*

Tony had committed suicide in three past lives and that energy was trying to manifest itself again in this life. The energy came into awareness now because he was deliberately working to clear up his restrictive life programs. The second reason was a benefit.

Q. *Do you want to kill yourself so you won't have to face life's problems? (+)*

Tony had to face the suicide program established in past lives and release the energy or risk the possibility of committing suicide again thus reinforcing the subconscious program. Then a future incarnation would be needed to face and work through the energy of suicide.

Q. *Any other reason for the desire to commit suicide? (-)*

We made the necessary releasing statements† and then checked to make certain the suicide program was clear. The following is reflective of the new programs we put into the subconscious mind.

Q. *Did you ever commit suicide in a former life? (-)*

Q. *Have you lived all past lives richly and fully and died of old age of natural causes? (+)*

Q. *Do you have a desire to commit suicide now? (-)*

Q. *Do you have a desire to live life fully and productively now? (+)*

Each week, when Tony returned for counseling, we checked to make certain he was still clear of the past life based desire to commit suicide. He has remained clear and his life this time around has taken on new meaning.

Case study #3:   Marriage difficulties

As ministers, my wife, Mary Ann, and I had always made it a practice of working with married couples two on two. Sometimes we were successful in bringing husband and wife closer together in a meaningful relationship and sometimes we were not. Our ratio of successes to failures was, perhaps, fifty percent. We always felt gratified, even if we could make the separation less painful for the couple. Since we began using Spiritual Response Therapy, our successes over our failures have improved significantly.

Ted and Sally came to us for counseling and as usual Mary Ann and I met with them as a couple. We asked them if they wanted their marriage to grow and Ted readily said he did. Sally was very hesitant and her "yes" answer was given seemingly with great reluctance. I told them I wanted to work with them individually and asked if they were agreeable to counsel that way. Again, Ted quickly said "yes" and Sally's "yes" was seemingly very reluctant. I scheduled an appointment with each of them; Sally was first. She sat down in the chair and said: "I want to get something very clear with you."

I said, "All right! What is it?"

These are, as near as I can remember, her next words.

"There is nothing you can do and nothing you can say to keep me with this man. I don't love him! I don't even like him! In fact, I can't stand him and I am not staying!"

I replied, "That is all right with me. I don't have any chips in the game. But do you want to clear up your subconscious programs, so if you wish to marry someone else later on, you won't run into the same problems?"

---

†Since High Self can clear all programs, releasing statements are not necessary, but they can be of great benefit in certain situations, as explained in Chapter 3.

Her reply was, "Yes, I want to work with you."

Sally was a good subject and we quickly determined the movements of the pendulum, asked our check questions and began work.

Ted and Sally had been married three years and were a beautiful couple. I had the privilege of performing their wedding service. One of the major problems in their relationship at the time they sought counseling was the lack of intimacy. During the three years of marriage they had had intercourse only four times. I could understand why they were having problems. There was a decided lack of closeness. The four times were: on their honeymoon, and once during each of their vacations over the next three years. This was a prime clue to the unfolding drama.

Q. *How many reasons are there for the discordant energy on Ted? (three)*

The first reason was an identification program; she identified with Ted. She saw Ted as lacking in assertiveness, introverted, and having low self-esteem. All of these were indicated as problems which were affecting their relationship in a discordant way. These programs were cleared and the new programs put in.

The next reason was a conflict program.

Q. *Do you want to love Ted but can't? (+)*

Q. *Do you love him? (+)*

Q. *Do you like him? (+)*

Q. *Are you in love with Ted? (-)*

Q. *Are you in conflict because Ted has poor eating habits and is overweight? (+)*

Q. *Is that a detriment to his health? (+)*

Q. *Any other reason of conflict? (-)*

Sally made the conscious statement that she neither liked nor loved Ted. However, questioning her subconscious mind revealed that she not only loved him, but liked him as well. What Sally consciously thought was the issue was not the real problem.

The third reason was a past life program where the real problem had its roots. Using the standard questioning method, we determined that three past lives were involved.

Past life number one:

Q. *Were you female? (+)*

Q. *Was Ted male? (+)*

Q. *Were you related? (+)*

Q. *Were you husband and wife? (-)*

Q. *Were you mother and son? (-)*

Q. *Were you father and daughter? (-)*

Q. *Were you brother and sister? (+) (The clue)*

Q. *Were you brother and sister in more than one life? (+)*

Q. *In all three? (+)*

Q. *Is that why you cannot have intercourse at home? (+)*

Q. *Is there any other reason we need to find? (-)*

These programs were cleared and a new program established. There was an immediate change in the relationship. I worked several sessions with Ted. We did not cover the same ground as these past lives. We did work on clearing his inability to communicate and some other problems. Now, when I ask them how they are doing, their eyes light up, they smile and say, "Great!" They have made some drastic changes by moving into a new house and replacing much of their furniture. Not only has their outer house been refurnished but their inner houses, the houses of consciousness, have been refurnished with new beliefs. "And a man's foes shall be they of his own household" (Matthew, 10:36). Realizing that we are beings of consciousness who live in the residence of our own minds and that we have given birth to many thought children, some of whom are evil (hurtful), helps us to understand, indeed, that our enemies are not out there in the world but in our own minds.

Case study #4:   Dislike of stepson

Bert could never understand why he intensely disliked his stepson. There was only one reason—a past life program.

Q. *What were you? (male)*

Q. *What was your stepson? (brother)*

Q. *Did he do something to hurt you? (+)*

Q. *Stole your girlfriend? (+)*

Q. *Was that your present wife and his mother now? (+)*

Q. *Did she become his wife in that life? (+)*

Q. *Are you fearful that he will steal her again? (+)*

Q. *Any other reason for the discordant energy on him? (-)*

Before we found and cleared this past life, Bert could not even stand to be around the stepson let alone be responsive to the child. Once the energy was dissolved, the whole situation changed. They were able to converse and even share some meaningful times together.

Case study #5: Self-destruction

Sue had ten percent positive and fifty percent discordant energy on herself. There were four reasons. The first was a benefit program which had its root in self-punishment. She felt she had to punish herself because she had not lived her life as she should. The next two reasons were conflict and self-punishment programs and both were centered in the benefit statement. The final reason was past life programs—six of them.

Life number one:

Q. *What were you? (female)*

Q. *Someone else involved? (+, husband) (At this point I felt a strong energy charge in the solar plexus).*

Q. *Was that man me? (+)*

Q. *Did I hurt or harm you in some way in that life? (+)*

Q. *Mentally/emotionally? (+)*

Q. *Physically? (-)*

Q. *I had an affair with another woman? (+)*

Q. *That made you feel like a failure and not worthwhile? (+)*

Q. *Did we have children? (+, nine)*

Q. *I blamed you for having so many children? (+)*

Q. *Was that my excuse for the affair with the other woman? (+)*

Q. *Anything else we need to find on this life? (-)*

Life number two:

Q. *Were you a soldier in the Civil War? (+)*

Q. *Did you feel guilty about killing the enemy? (+)*

Q. *Did you feel you were a coward? (+)*

Q. *Did you run away? (+)*

Q. *Were you captured and tortured by the enemy? (+)*

Q. *Did you lose your life then? (+)*

Q. *Were you a failure in that life? (+)*

Q. *Anything else we need to find on that lifetime? (-)*

Life number three:

Q. *What were you? (female)*

Q. *Any one else involved? (+, husband)*

Q. *Did you emotionally harm him? (+)*

Q. *Anything else on life number three? (-)*

Life number four:

Q. *What were you? (female)*

Q. *Someone else involved? (-)*

Q. *Were you a member of a religious order? (+)*

Q. *Was this life in India? (+)*

Q. *You felt restricted as a woman? (+)*

Q. *Unable to do all you wanted to do for others? (+)*

Q. *Anything else we need to know? (-)*

Life number five:

Q. *What were you? (male)*

Q. *Someone else involved? (+, wife) (She is her sister in this life.)*

Q. *Someone else involved? (+, female)*

Q. *Was she your mother then and now? (+)*

Q. *Did your wife hurt you in that life? (+)*

Q. *Did she leave you and go to her mother? (+)*

Q. *You were stuck with all of the children? (+)*

Q. *Did that make life difficult for you? (+)*

Q. *Anything else we need to know about this life? (-)*

Life number six:

Q. *What were you? (male)*

Q. *Was someone else involved? (-)*

Q. *Were you a member of a religious order in India? (+)*

Q. *Were you cast out of the order because of your rebellion? (+)*

Q. *Anything else we need to know? (-)*

Finding all of this past life information was made much simpler because Sue had some psychic ability. The moment we identified the people involved, she tuned in on the past life and told me what she remembered. All we had to do was confirm what she was seeing by having her hold the pendulum while I asked questions. How Sue expressed and what she experienced in this life was strongly influenced by her past lives. She seemed to be living more from the energy of the past than in the present.

We worked on a fear of success program that involved twelve past lives. They were a complete series of cosmic soap operas. All twelve were extremely traumatic and involved her committing suicide in three of them. Sue was doing a good job of destroying her life this time around also. Thanks to Spiritual Response Therapy all of that has changed and Sue has at last found peace of mind, self-assurance, and a positive direction in her life. The most gratifying result is that she is no longer seeking to destroy or even to limit her life in any way.

Case study #6:   Excess weight

Remember Iris and her weight problem from previous chapters? One of her past lives influenced the excess weight problem.

Q. *What were you? (female)*

Q. *Someone else involved? (+, mother)*

Iris was also very psychic and tuned in to each past life as soon as we identified the characters. These were just the confirmation questions:

Q. *Was this in the days of oil lamps? (+)*

Q. *Did your mother die? (+)*

Q. *Was she very fat? (+)*

Q. *Did you render the body for the oil to use in the lamps? (+)*

Q. *Are you punishing yourself for that in this life by being obese? (+)*

Q. *Anything else we need to know about this life? (-)*

Case study #7:   Physical abuse by son

The interpersonal relations between two people are often impacted by past lives. Here is a mother and son who had a lot of discordant energy in their current relationship that was a carry over from former lives. Diane had ninety percent positive and forty percent discordant energy on her son. A situation had arisen involving another member of the family and the son had physically abused his mother as a result. He had subsequently threatened her life and she had him arrested. When she set up her

counseling appointment with me, he was still in jail. However, he was soon to be released and she was fearful that he would seek to carry out his threat to harm her. Diane came to me hoping to find out why there seemed to be such anger and discordant energy between the two of them. There were ten reasons and we began with the identification program. Diane saw her son as being: arrogant, strong-willed, stubborn, frightened, crazy, abusive, frustrated, and unfulfilled. On the positive side, he was handsome and bright. Diane saw herself as arrogant, strong-willed, stubborn, frustrated, and unfulfilled.

There were three imprints. The first one was made when her son was four. She told herself that he was not a nice person and he embarrassed her. This first imprint was indicated to have had its roots in a past life. The second imprint was made on his tenth birthday. She told herself that her son was a selfish brat. The third imprint was made when he was fourteen years of age and she told herself he was unloving and vindictive.

Conflict was involved in all of the previously revealed information as well as one other message. Diane and her son loved each other, but they had a mutual dislike of each other. Many times, when working with people, I find that the client may love the person we are clearing, but they may not like them. Or they may see the other person as loving them, but not liking them.

The reason of experience/trauma was established at the time of birth. The birth of her son put her life in jeopardy. As we began to work with the past lives that were impacting their relationship, it soon became apparent that the relationship had been in jeopardy long before this present incarnation together. The energies that had been established between them in past lives needed to be cleared. So they designed another lifetime to work together in an attempt to face and release the problem areas that had caused them to abuse each other in previous lives. It was time to clear it all.

There were eight past lives that had a bearing on the current relationship. Only the questions to which we received "yes" responses are listed below, except where the "no" responses are pertinent to a full understanding of the case.

First past life:

Q. *What were you? (wife)*

Q. *What was he? (husband)*

Q. *Did he do something to abuse you? (+)*

Q. *Did he abuse you physically? (+)*

Q. *Did he kill you? (+)*

Q. *Anything else we need to know? (-)*

Second past life:

Q. *What were you? (mother)*

Q. *What was he? (son)*

Q. *Did you desert him? (+)*

Third past life:

Q. *What were you? (son)*

Q. *What was he? (mother)*

Q. *Did he desert you? (+)*

Fourth past life:

Q. *What were you? (mother)*

Q. *What was he? (son)*

Q. *Did he physically abuse you? (+)*

Q. *Did he kill you? (+)*

Fifth past life:

Q. *What were you? (male)*

Q. *What was he? (brother) (More specifically, they were stepbrothers.)*

Q. *Is there someone else involved? (+, female)*

Q. *Your mother and his stepmother? (+)*

Q. *She loved you and not your stepbrother? (+)*

Q. *Were you self-righteous about that? (+)*

Q. *Did it cause conflict between you? (+)*

Sixth past life:

Q. *What were you? (female)*

Q. *What was he? (male)*

Q. *He was your servant? (+)*

Q. *Did you physically harm him? (+)*

Q. *Did you kill him? (+)*

Seventh past life:

Q. *What were you? (female)*

Q. *What was your son? (female)*

Q. *Someone else involved? (+, male)*

Q. *Were they husband and wife? (+)*

Q. *Did you steal him from your son? (+)*

Q. *Is that person in this life? (+)*

Q. *Is it P...? (+)*

Eighth past life:

Q. *What were you? (male)*

Q. *What was your son? (male)*

Q. *Were you monks in a religious order? (+)*

Q. *Were you friends? (+)*

Q. *Was jealousy involved? (+)*

Q. *On both your parts? (+)*

Q. *Did you harm him by accusing him of heresy? (+)*

Q. *Did you cause him to be put to death? (+)*

This is a perfect example of energies that were established in previous lives being resolved in the current life. Jealousy, hate, death, desertion, and many other forms of hurt are involved. These lives explain the Old Testament law of "an eye for an eye, and a tooth for a tooth." They each deserted the other once and they each killed the other or at least caused their death twice. Obviously, what goes around on the wheel of life comes around again. In this present life they have the opportunity to either add to the discordant energy that has been accumulating between them or they may release, forgive and set each other free. Freedom comes when we know the truth and deliberately work with a consciousness of love and forgiveness. The energy between Diane and her son has dramatically changed although I did not work with him. He is probably completely unaware that I even worked with her.

CHAPTER 18

Past Lives In Other Dimensions

As previously stated, the subconscious mind differentiates between past lives on Earth and past lives in other dimensions. This results in a strange anomaly about past lives. Unless you believe in past lives in other dimensions, or are open to greater levels of spiritual awareness, they will not show up as a cause for any problem—even if the only way to clear the program is to realize that the past life was in another dimension. The first case study in this chapter illustrates this perfectly.

High Self has indicated that body forms on other planets differ from those on Earth and that people in some other dimensions may not have physical forms as we understand physical forms. Bodies seem to be more spiritual.

My High Self has revealed that if and when men from Earth go to other planets, they may or may not find life as we know it here on Earth because life could be at a different vibratory level or different dimension. This is not to infer that every planet throughout infinite space would have life in other dimensions or vibrations and none exactly like Earth. There are many planets with vibrations similar to Earth and if we were capable of going there, we would see those life forms even as we see our own.

Some people have had lives in the constellation Pleiades and this is where a decided difference from Earth lives is encountered. The first time I worked with someone with past lives in this constellation, a very strange movement of the pendulum was received. When we asked if they were female, the pendulum would swing in a short "yes" movement and then switch to a short "no" movement. It continued to move in the same manner when asked if they had been

male in that life. Next I asked:

Q. *Were you both male and female in that life? (+)*

Q. *Are people on the planet where you lived androgynous? (+)*

Whenever I get a "no" response to both sexes in a past life in other dimensions, I ask if it is a life in the Pleiades. Invariably the answer is "yes." There are probably places other than Pleiades where the form of life is androgynous, but I have not discovered them yet.

One thing is certain, interactions between two souls in other dimensions are similar to those on Earth. Regardless of the dimension, there is love and hate, peace and anger, life and death, pain and joy. All souls appear to go through repeated cycles of positive and discordant energy wherever they choose to incarnate. The schoolrooms may vary, but the lessons always seem to be the same. If the whole purpose of life energies (at least from what I have found to date) could be put into one concise sentence, it would be: "Love or suffer." Jesus put it into a very simple, but profound statement, "A new commandment I give unto you, that you love one another; even as I have loved you, that you also love one another" (John, 13:34).

Technique

To research programs of past lives in other dimensions, use the standard technique as explained in Chapter 7. Since body forms differ in other dimensions, all the possibilities of how they may actually appear could not be put on Chart 3. So you may get a response of androgynous simply because a more accurate response is not available on the chart. The true body type is usually not important to understanding the circumstances. Just ask the standard questions (who harmed whom and what the energies were, etc.) and that should provide all the information needed to clear the program.

Case study #1: Arthritis

Miriam had gone through several hours of Response Therapy with the people who taught me. Part of their research was aimed at clearing up a severe case of rheumatoid arthritis. After the clearing work was done, there did not seem to be much change in the condition of her body. She came to me desperate for a solution. Since she was already set up to use a pendulum, I started asking questions:

Q. *Is there any reason for you to have arthritis? (-)*

Q. *Do you have arthritis? (-)*

Knowing that she was experiencing a great amount of pain because of an arthritic condition and her subconscious mind was not giving right answers, I asked for and received permission to ask questions through my High Self. As I pointed out in Chapter 4, there were six reasons for the problem and the area was past lives in other dimensions.

There are many similarities between past lives on planet Earth and past lives in other dimensions. There are also decided differences and these differences caused me considerable confusion until I began to understand them more fully. Here, you can see how Miriam's lives on Venus were similar to Earth lives.

Q. *Were these lives in our solar system? (+)*

Q. *Were they on Venus? (+)*

Life number one:

Q. *What were you? (female)*

Q. *Was someone else involved? (+, husband)*

Q. *Anyone else involved? (+)*

Q. *A child? (+)*

Q. *Is there more than one child involved? (+, four)*

Q. *Did you do something to harm them? (+)*

Q. *Did you harm them physically? (+)*

Q. *Was it death by fire? (+)*

Q. *Did you set the fire deliberately? (+)*

Q. *Anything else we need to know? (-)*

Life number two

Q. *What were you? (female)*

Q. *Was there someone else involved? (husband)*

Q. *Were there any children involved? (+)*

When I started asking if anyone else was involved, the answer was always "yes" and each time it turned out to be a child. This led to the following question:

Q. *How many children are there? (254) (Again, we used the chart and questions to find the number of children.)*

Q. *Was this an orphanage? (+)*

Q. *Was fire involved in this life? (+)*

Q. *Did you set the fire? (-)*

Q. *Did you feel responsible? (+)*

Her husband and fifty-six children died in the fire.

Life number three

Q. *What were you? (wife)*

Q. *A male involved in that life? (+, husband)*

Q. *Any children involved? (+, four)*

Q. *Did you kill them? (+)*

Q. *Were their deaths caused by fire? (+)*

Q. *Did you deliberately set the fire? (+)*

Life number four

Q. *What were you? (wife)*

Q. *Was there a male involved? (+, husband)*

Q. *Were there any children involved? (+, one)*

Q. *Was there death by fire again? (+)*

Q. *Was it deliberate? (+)*

Life number five

Q. *What were you? (male)*

Q. *Was there a female involved? (+, wife)*

Q. *Did you cause your spouse pain? (+)*

Q. *Did you die of a high fever? (+)*

Life number six

Q. *What were you? (daughter)*

Q. *Was there someone else involved? (+, father)*

Q. *Did you do something to hurt your father? (+)*

Q. *Did you die of a high fever? (+)*

Q. *How old were you? (seven)*

Q. *You hurt your father by dying? (+)*

Q. *Was I your father in that life? (+)*

This is another case in which I had a high energy feeling in the solar plexus, and guessed that I might be involved. There is a strong feeling of closeness between me and the client in this life and I feel toward her as I do toward my own daughter.

Q. *Is self-punishment involved with all of these past lives? (+)*

Q. *Anything else we need to know about these past lives? (-)*

Q. *Anything else causing the arthritis? (-)*

Q. *Is there a correlation between the inflammation (arthritis) in this life and the deaths by flames (fire) and the pain caused through dying of flames in past lives? (+)*

The specific situations found on other planets (at least on Venus), as reported by Miriam's subconscious mind, are similar to those here on Earth.

Case study #2: Discordant energy on mother

Ruth (see the chapter on imprints) had discordant energy on her mother because she saw God as her real mother and her earthly mother would not let her die and go home. Based on eight past lives in other dimensions, Ruth had one hundred percent discordant and only ten percent positive energy on herself with a desire to die and return to God, her Mother.

Life number one

Q. *What were you? (female)*

Q. *Was there someone else involved? (+, husband)*

Q. *Did you fail him in some way? (+)*

Q. *Did you fail to give him children? (+)*

Q. *Did you die in childbirth? (+)*

Q. *Anything else we need to know about this life? (-)*

Life number two

Q. *What were you? (female)*

Q. *Was there someone else involved? (+, male)*

Q. *Were they related? (-)*

Q. *Was there someone else involved? (+, male)*

Q. *Were they related? (-)*

Q. *Was there someone else involved? (-)*

Q. *Did you do something to hurt them? (+)*

Q. *Did you lead them on and then reject them? (+)*

Q. *Anything else we need to know about this life? (+)*

Q. *Do we need to know who these men are in this life? (+)*

Further questioning revealed that they were her fiancee, Tony, and a male cousin.

Life number three

Q. *What were you? (female)*

Q. *Was there someone else involved? (-)*

Q. *Did you harm yourself in that life. (+, suicide)*

Q. *Were you despondent? (+)*

Q. *Did you feel separate from God? (+)*

Q. *Were you psychic? (+)*

Q. *Did you fail to use your psychic gifts? (+)*

Q. *Did you kill yourself because you wanted to go back to God? (+)*

Life number four

Q. *What were you? (wife)*

Q. *Was there someone else involved? (+, husband)*

Q. *Was there someone else involved? (+, mother)*

Q. *Were there a lot of people involved? (+)*

Q. *Were you psychic? (+)*

Q. *Did the people kill you? (+)*

Q. *Did your husband and mother betray you? (+)*

Q. *Anything else we need to know about this life? (+)*

Q. *Do we need to know who these people are in this life? (+)*

Additional questioning revealed that the past life husband was a former boy friend in this life. The past life mother is the father in this life.

Life number five

Q. *What were you? (+, female)*

Q. *Was there someone else involved? (-)*

Q. *Did you harm yourself in that life? (+, suicide)*

Q. *Is this a carbon copy of life number three? (+)*

Q. *Are there any more carbon copy lives? (+, two)*

Q. *There were a total of five lives where you killed yourself in order to return to God? (+)*

Q. *Is that why you wanted to die in this life, so you could fulfill your desire to return to God? (+)*

In almost every past life investigated, there were a number of people involved who are members of her family now or who are close friends.

CHAPTER 19

Future Lives

છ૦ ભ

Is it true that there is no time and space? From the results of working with clients in Spiritual Response Therapy, it appears to be true. Future lives fall under three headings—lives being lived right now, lives that are completely planned but not being lived and lives that are in the planning stage.

Although our awareness is limited to the now expression of the current life, it soon becomes apparent that there is much more to life than meets the eye. Einstein's theory of relativity has shown that space and time are not absolute. As human beings we have come to know that consciousness and energy are one and all of space is constructed by consciousness or ideas moving into being. Thus, through Spiritual Response Therapy, our normal perception of reality becomes a composite of an indefinite number of lives lived in indefinite levels of awareness and on many planets (in this galaxy and others) and without sequential time of past, present, and future.

Like past lives, future lives cannot be proven. However, if there is a change in the life energy of a person as a result of clearing future lives, it is well worth the time to work with the subconscious mind with the assumption that there may well be future lives that are affecting the present.

Technique

To research future lives programs, use the standard procedure as explained in Chapter 7.

Since it appears that we will be living future lives, even as we have lived past lives, we want to set the future lives up with good energy. The best way to clear future lives is to have your High Self do the work rather than using releasing statements. High Self knows exactly how to clear the lives without setting up more energy that has to be dealt with later.†

Case study #1: Future lives revealed

While working with a female client, Faith, on the discordant energy she had on her mother, we ran across future lives. First, we used a chart with numbers to find the time a certain energy was established—we came up with nothing. Then I began to ask questions:

Q. *Did this take place before you were five?* (-)

Q. *Did this take place after you were five?* (-)

Q. *Did this take place before you were born?* (-)

Q. *Did it take place during the Bardo?* (-) (The Bardo is the period between lives when you review your record and determine what you need to do in the next life.)

Q. *Did this take place in a past life?* (-)

Q. *Did it take place in other dimensions?* (-)

Running out of things to ask, I took a stab in the dark.

Q. *Are we dealing with a future life.* (+)

Q. *Is this a life that you are living at the present time?* (+)

---

†All of the clients who's case studies are included in this chapter came for counseling before I had learned how to work with my High Self committee. Since High Self can clear future life programs and replace them with good without creating any more situations that have to be dealt with later, I now simply ask High Self to "clear and replace with good" rather than use releasing statements.

Case study #2: Number of planned lives increases

When I first started working with George, he had two future lives planned, neither of which were being lived, and one on the drawing board but not completed. After a lot of clearing work with George, the number of lives completely planned started to increase and we began to find energy on some that were being lived now.

Case study #3: Discordant energy on boyfriend

Arlene wanted to clear the sixty-five percent discordant energy on her boyfriend.

Q. What is the reason for this discordant energy? (future lives - using chart and pendulum)

Q. Is it a reason of future lives? (+)

Q. Are you living the future life now? (+)

Q. What are you? (male)

Q. What is he? (wife)

Q. Is there someone else involved? (+)

Q. Are they female? (+)

Q. Are they related? (+)

Q. What is the relationship to you?

Arlene said, "She is my daughter, but she is not my daughter."

Q. Is this female a blood relative of yours? (-)

Q. Is she your wife's child? (+)

Q. Did your wife have a child by another man? (+)

Q. Is that why you have discordant energy on your boyfriend now? (+)

Q. Is there anything else we need to know about this future life? (-)

We wanted to clear this future life, but questioned how to handle it without setting up more karma than was cleared.

Q. Can we release belief, perception and judgment that this is not your child? (+)

Q. Will this cause more karma? (+)

Q. Can we set it up so that you know that the child is not your child, but you completely accept her as your daughter and raise her with love and in harmony with the mother (the current boyfriend) of the child? (+)

Q. Will this cause any bad karma? (-)

Q. Is this the way we should do it for the greatest good of all concerned? (+)

Sensing that there might be some reason for the daughter being born as the child of another man, I asked:

Q. Is there a past life connection with this child? (+)

Q. Was this child rejected by you in a previous life? (+)

Q. Is that why she must not be rejected in the future life, but completely accepted and raised in harmony and love? (+)

Case study #4: Painful friendship

Ada, Biddy, and Cindy are twelve years old. Ada and Biddy had a close relationship starting in the second or third grade. The relationship became a threesome when Cindy became a mutual friend in the sixth grade. There were times when Biddy did not want Ada to have anything to do with Cindy. She informed Ada that they could not be friends if Ada wanted to be friends with Cindy. However, Biddy threw a party for Ada when she moved from Southern California to the Bay area and all seemed to be well between them.

A few months later Ada visited Cindy and when Biddy appeared on the scene she told Ada (who was just leaving) that she had been there long enough. During the Christmas season, Ada wrote to Biddy apologizing for whatever she had done to Biddy and asked that they be friends. The answering letter that came from Biddy was very vindictive and stated that they could never be friends. It was this letter that brought Ada to me for counseling. Ada could not understand what she had done to Biddy to cause her to be so angry and hostile.

The first reason was past life programs. During the first one, Ada was the stepmother of Biddy, a male child, and Cindy was his mother. There was an accident in which Ada caused her stepson (Biddy) mental, emotional and physical harm. Although it was not serious hurt, it started the problems in subsequent lives and led to the current problems in this life.

During the second past life, Ada was female and was in love with Cindy who was Biddy's father. Biddy came between them causing mental and emotional trauma for Ada. Ada was so hurt in that life that she committed suicide.

The next life revealed Biddy as a female servant to Ada, who's son was Cindy. Biddy sexually molested the son (Cindy) starting when he was one year old and continuing until he was five, at which time Ada found out about the molestation. She promptly had Biddy beheaded.

The fourth life with the three together was also traumatic. Ada and Biddy were brothers. Both were in love with Cindy who was the wife of another man. Both were trying to take Cindy away from her husband and Biddy killed him. Cindy ended up rejecting both Ada and Biddy.

The next reason for discordant energy was an organ language program in which Biddy implied that Ada was too thin.

Q. *Is there another reason causing the problem of discordant energy between the three of you? (+)*

Q. *What is the area? (future lives - using chart and pendulum)*

Q. *Are you living that life now? (+)*

Q. *What are you? (female)*

Q. *What is Biddy? (male)*

Q. *Are you related? (-)*

Q. *What is Cindy? (female, and sister)*

Q. *Are you and Biddy sweethearts? (+)*

Q. *Does Biddy leave you for Cindy? (+)*

Q. *Is that a reason for discordant energy on Biddy? (+)*

Q. *Is there any other reason for discordant energy between you? (-)*

I discussed the various possibilities of releasing this discordant energy and setting up new positive energies with Ada and asked her what she would like to do regarding this future life. She stated that she would prefer releasing Biddy and Cindy from any discordant energy by allowing them to come together in a positive loving union as husband and wife with her complete love and full support.

Q. *Can it be done this way? (+)*

Q. *Would it cause any additional problems? (-)*

Q. *Would this be best for all concerned? (+)*

Q. *Would doing this dissolve all of the discordant energy between them? (+)*

I led Ada in the releasing statements as suggested by her inner self. She went home and burned the letter that Biddy had sent. She has completely released the situation and is at peace knowing that things will work out perfectly as long as she is loving and forgiving.

Case study #5:   Back problem

Self punishment was the major reason for Wanda's back problem. The first reason was an organ language program which had its inception in the Bardo. She planned to come in to life and experience a back problem. The self-punishment had its roots in past lives. In the first life, she accidentally caused her husband a serious back injury. In the next life, she suffered a back injury and had a hard time handling it. This resulted in a mental break down which was her way of escaping the pain. Guilt over not facing the pain set up the self-punishment program.

During the third life there was some rather interesting energy. The other characters were: her brother (who is her father now), a sister, and an unrelated woman. Wanda was a psychic and taught her brother the art. He perverted the art into black magic and the other two were involved with him. Wanda felt she had created a monster. She felt responsible for what was being done and exposed the three of them. They broke her back and killed her. The energy of self-punishment was set up because she blamed herself for creating a monster.

Wanda was a spiritual leader (psychic) in the next life with a lot of followers. She, along with her followers, was imprisoned. They were tortured on the rack and Wanda had a soul memory of her back being broken. Since she felt responsible for the torture and death of her followers, she set up another self-punishment program.

The future life had only one other character—a grandfather who was Wanda's grandmother in the present life.

Q. *Are you living this future life now? (+)*

Q. *Do you hurt your grandfather in the future life? (+)*

Q. *Is it a back problem? (+)*

Q. *Should you be taking care of him in that life? (+)*

Q. *Do you refuse to take care of him? (+)*

Q. *Should you have taken care of your grandmother in this life? (+)*

Q. *Do you blame yourself for her death? (+)*

Q. *Is there anything else we need to know about this life? (-)*

Q. *Is there self-punishment involved with the future life? (+)*

Q. *Is it involved with your present back problem? (+)*

We had to clear the guilt about Wanda's feeling that she had not taken care of her grandmother and had caused her death in this life, as well as the energy of self-punishment from the future life.

Case study #6: Fear of ex-boyfriend

Ruth's moving to New York City, which was her original home, caused her to experience a lot of fear and uneasiness due of a former boyfriend. Although she did not see him upon her return to New York City, the energy between them was surfacing.

There were four reasons for the discordant energy on Victor: imprint, past lives in other dimensions, self-punishment, and trauma programs. The trauma occurred fifteen years before when Victor tried to strangle her. The self-punishment was set up during December of 1979 when she was in relationship with Victor a second time. There was also a self-punishment program that led to past lives. In the first and third lives, Victor had killed Ruth. During past life number two, Victor, whom she believed was her friend, broke up her relationship with a man who is today her cousin. Investigation of the final life revealed that she was spiritually inclined and Victor thwarted her spiritual expression because of his jealousy. Her reason for the self-punishment was that she had made a mistake in trusting him.

The dynamics of the first past life in other dimensions was one of a power struggle between them which he won. Again, he hurt her spiritually by thwarting her psychic abilities and she caused him physical injuries. They were both psychic and Victor used his abilities in promoting the black arts.

The second past life in other dimensions found Victor using his abilities in a dark way. He used his power to kill Ruth during a power struggle between good and evil. They were good friends and Ruth felt sad because of the struggle between them.

Investigating life number three we found that Victor hurt Ruth mentally and emotionally because he again turned from the path of Spirit. She felt that he was holding her back from her own spiritual progress because they are soul mates and he is doing nothing about his own spiritual growth. Ruth's major fear in that life and in this one was that she would have to be incarnated with him again. During that past life in other dimensions he had said that he would get even with her.

When we looked at the reason of imprint, this is what we found.

Q. *Is this imprint something you told yourself? (+)*

Q. *When did you give yourself this imprint? (future lives)*

Q. *Are you living this life now? (+)*

Q. *What were you? (female)*

Q. *What is Victor? (male)*

Q. *Are you related? (-)*

Q. *Does he harm you in some way? (+)*

Q. *Is there physical harm? (+)*

Q. *Is it serious harm? (+)*

Q. *Does Victor kill you? (+)*

Q. *Is there anything else we need to know about this life? (+)*

Q. *What is the energy involved? (unforgiveness, Chart 4)*

Q. *Did you tell yourself you would never love or forgive him? (+)*

Q. *Is there anything else we need to know about this life? (-)*

We used releasing statements[†] to clear all of this and put in statements of forgiveness, life, love, friendship, and that he cared for and protected her from all harm. A check showed that the energy had been changed and the discordant energy dissolved. We were assured by her subconscious mind and by my High Self that everything was all right between them in the future life and no discordant energy was set up.

---

†Since High Self can clear all programs, releasing statements are not necessary, but they can be of great benefit in certain situations, as explained in Chapter 3.

Case study #7: Laryngitis

Florence, a professional executive, had been experiencing several days of laryngitis. By the time she came to see me, she realized that the laryngitis was part of a repeat pattern of her life. Many years before, in a marriage that suffered because of a lack of communication, throat problems were a yearly occurrence. Florence felt that the laryngitis was caused by her being unable to express her feelings, and thus, giving away her power of speech. She realized that the throat was the seat of her ability to emote and express herself in a meaningful way. If she could not talk, she could not be worthwhile.

Although Florence was now involved in a good marriage, she still didn't know how to express her own power through her speech. Since her profession involved public speaking, it was vitally important for Florence to be clear from any blocks that would cause her speech difficulties. Several months prior to working with me, she had experienced an inner drive to share publicly her deepest feelings and began to freely exhibit more emotion in public. That stirred up old subconscious programming and several weeks before the laryngitis started, her speech began to change. She developed a pattern of repeating short phrases and words several times before she would complete a sentence. This was so unusual, that she decided to work with Spiritual Response Therapy and find out what was causing the repetition of words.

The first program was five past lives with her soul mate (her father in this life) where she totally subjugated her feminine self to his dominant male personality. It was necessary to research two of these past lives. In the first life, Florence was killed for speaking out for the rights of herself and other women in a strict Calvinist community. Her soul mate was one of the male authority figures that killed her. Research of the fourth past life, showed her soul mate as her husband to whom she was totally submissive, giving up her ability to express herself.

Another reason was a conflict program. Florence wanted to express herself completely but was afraid of being ridiculed and thought of as stupid. These energies of conflict had their roots in the five past lives.

The most interesting reason was a program of nine future lives. The future life she was living now dealt with the relationship of the sexes and the need for equal communication for females in relationship to men. Florence is a leader and trend setter of social mores in the future life and is very much in the public eye. In six other future lives that she is living now, the same theme is repeated where she is a leader seeking to improve and upgrade feminine communication and recognition.

The remaining two future lives are planned to deal with the theme of personal integrity and the ability to fully and freely express the emotions and project the self honestly and openly without interference, subterfuge, or manipulation. No clearing was necessary on these future lives.

As a result of our clearing work, the speech patterns changed immediately, the laryngitis cleared up and she is able to freely express her deepest convictions and feelings without fear of ridicule.

CHAPTER 20

Fear

ဆ ⚬ ⚬ ひ

There are many kinds of fear and almost everyone has one or more. There is fear of success, fear of failure, fear of heights, fear of falling, fear of water, fear of crowds, fear of being alone, fear of spiders, snakes, dogs, etc., to name just a few. They can have their inception in this life or in any other life all the way back to the beginning of time when only the GODHEAD existed.

Technique

To research fear programs, use the standard technique as explained in Chapter 7.

Case study #1:   Fears and phobias

Marta had a devastating fear of snakes. As a ten year old female in a past life, Marta was bitten by a cobra and died a very painful death. Questioning revealed that she had been harmed by serpents in 437 lives. Marta also had an all consuming fear of spiders. She was bitten by spiders in 1,058 lives and suffered death 92 times. Claustrophobia was another of her fears and we found she had been buried alive in 204 lives

CHAPTER 21

Discarnates

ॐ ॐ

A discarnate is a person who has left the physical body through death but has not departed the Earth. There are many reasons why a discarnate does not leave the Earth. They may stay because they have a strong tie to a person still living. They may not realize they are dead. They may be addicted to drugs, alcohol, sex, food, etc. They may be fearful of punishment or of retribution from God or someone they have injured. They may not believe in an afterlife, so they are staying here. There are even some who stay here for revenge. Since they have no physical bodies of their own, they attach themselves to the living, who do have bodies, in an attempt to satisfy their needs. Whatever the reason, they can cause problems for the person who becomes a host.

Discarnates affect the host in a variety of ways and seldom are they positive or beneficial. One person who had discarnates said they were beneficial to her. When I asked High Self if they were beneficial, I received a "yes" response. When I asked if they should be released anyway, another "yes" response was received. The client gave her permission and they were sent on.

The host may pick up the symptoms and eventually the condition that the discarnate had manifested while in the physical body. The condition might be as simple as an addiction to chocolate, or as major as an addiction to cocaine. The discarnates may cause obesity in the host through compulsive overeating. At the very least, the discarnates set up crosscurrents of energy and almost everyone I work with,

when discarnates are released, notices an immediate increase in their energy level.

Clients often want to know when they picked up the unwanted tenants and are surprised to find (through questioning High Self) that it may have happened at birth. The soul who picks up discarnates at birth may have a difficult time living life in a constructive or meaningful manner because of the conflicting energy of the discarnates.

There are several types of discarnates, some more negative than others. As they are listed on Chart 1 from the left to the right, the discordant energies and negative attitudes of the souls get progressively worse. High Self can clear all of them—if the person is willing to be free.[†]

Discarnates in the Aura or in Possession

Discarnates in the aura and in possession are what I call simple discarnates. They are your average run of discarnate souls who get stuck in the earth vibrations and they have little or no discordant energy. Nevertheless, I ask High Self to clear every client of all discarnates regardless of type. I then check to make certain all of them have been removed.

Discarnates in Past Lives

When a past life is opened, discarnates from that past life may come into the current time and cause problems. This is also true of past lives in other dimensions and parallel lives. It is sometimes difficult for people to understand

---

†All of the clients whose case studies are included in this chapter came for counseling before I had learned how to work with my High Self committee. Since High Self can clear all discarnates and extra souls, now I simply ask High Self to "clear and replace with good" rather than do the work as explained in this chapter.

or believe that opening another life can cause the discarnate souls involved to come into the current time. I explain to them that in Spirit and in truth there is no such thing as time and space, and when you open up the past life, to all intent and purpose, you are living it now. Just as when you regress someone under hypnosis, they actually relive the events as though they are occurring now.

Satanics and Demonics

Satanics are discarnates with bad energies, and demonics have worse energies.

Dark Energies

A dark energy is any discarnate soul who is carrying some dark energy. For examples of dark energies refer to the energies listed on Chart 4. These energies are all discordant and considered by High Self to be dark energies.

Dark Forces, Satanic Forces and Demonic Forces

Dark forces is a group of souls with dark energy. A satanic force is a group of satanics, and a demonic force is a group of demonics.

Healthy Physical and Auric Vibrations

The normal vibration of a healthy person (according to my High Self) is 2,100 cycles per second. Anything that lowers the body vibration sufficiently leaves the person open to possession by discarnates. In the early 1920s Georges Lakhovsky, a Russian-born engineer living in Paris, had begun a series of books which suggested that the basis of life was not matter but immaterial vibrations associated with it. Every living thing emits radiations," stressed Lakhovsky (as quoted in *"The Secret Life of Plants"* by Peter Tompkins and Christopher Bird). In the same book, Simoneton is quoted as stating that a healthy person gives off a radiance of 6,500 angstroms or a little higher. In discussing microscopic organisms the book suggests that:

> *From the fact that most microbes read well below 6.5 thousand angstroms, Simoneton, deduces that microbes can only affect a human being whose vitality has been lowered to a point where cells resonate at their wavelength, whereas a body with a healthy vitality remains immune to attack by microbes.*

The same principle applies to discarnates and their ability to invade the body of a person or their aura (energy field around the body). Unless the body and/or auric vibrations are lowered sufficiently, no discarnates can enter. Questioning my High Self revealed that the energy of a vitally whole body vibrates at 2,100 cycles per second, the same as the aura. A discarnate's normal vibration is 600 to 700 cycles per second. Therefore, any person that maintains their body and auric energy above 800 cycles is safe from possession. In your daily prayers, or at any time throughout the day, ask your High Self to raise your vibration to the maximum beneficial vibrations per second.

Causes of Lowered Vibrations

The physical and auric vibrations are lowered by any negative emotion, such as anger, guilt, and fear and by destructive habits. Additionally, a person may have programs which result in a lowered vibration or programs that make them susceptible to discarnates or possession. Or, they may have set up contracts requiring them to be a host. Any situation involving discarnates can be cleared and healed by High Self. With Spirit's help, no one ever needs to bear the burden of interference from discarnates.

Grief and Shock

Through questioning the subconscious minds of clients, it was revealed that grief and shock both lower the vibration of the body and leave a person open to possession. People who visit sick friends and relatives in a hospital are often in a state of grief or shock. Their body vibrations may be affected to the point that they are open to possession. Because death occurs in hospitals, there are usually a lot of discarnates in the vicinity who will attach themselves to any host that is open. People visiting hospitals may be vulnerable to invasion. My friend, who helped me clear the discarnates from Nancy (case study #5, below), is so sensitive that she sometimes became aware, after going to the hospital to visit her ill husband, that she had discarnates hanging around her. Sensing that they were there, she would question her High Self to make certain that what she was feeling was correct and then go through a clearing process to get rid of them.

Funerals, Cemeteries, and Memorial Services

By questioning other clients who have discarnates, I discovered that funerals are another place where it is easy to pick them up. This is especially true if the funeral is held in a facility connected to a cemetery.

There are times when the departed soul refuses to leave and simply attaches itself to some member of the family and goes home with them as an unseen, but not always unfelt, house guest. I have talked to many people who knew that their dear departed had not departed, but were with them and causing problems. Since guilt often accompanies the loss of a family member, friend or acquaintance, even when there may be no grief, sorrow or shock, it, too, can leave a person open to possession by the deceased, as can a desire to complete the work or some aspect of the life of the person who made their transition. However, regardless of the motivation, relationship or emotions involved, there is never any need to be a host for a discarnate of any kind.

Since I have become aware of the possibility that the departed soul may decide to stay in the earth realm, I have taken pains to make certain the deceased leaves by doing a simple but powerful releasing prayer near the end of every memorial service at which I officiate. Then I ask the family to join with me in a silent moment of prayer as we release the loved one into the light.

If you are going to be in the vicinity of a hospital or cemetery or need to attend a memorial service, ask your High Self to clear the area and everyone there of discarnates before you arrive and again as you leave. One client, Beth, who is sensitive to the presence of discarnates, never goes anywhere without asking High Self to clear the area of discarnates before she arrives. In fact, many times each day, wherever she is, she asks High Self to clear the area and all the Earth of all discarnates. She has learned the hard way through many struggles with discarnates that it is easier to just stay free of them. Beth is most grateful to be clear of the programs which caused her to be an inviting host to discarnates and is even more grateful

to be clear of all her programs so that she is able to not only trust, but to know, that Spirit does indeed do as she requests.

Alcohol and Drugs

Alcohol and drugs, even prescription drugs, can lower the vibration. And, as with cemeteries, there seems to be more discarnates wherever liquor is served, including restaurants. Since these discarnates often were alcoholics while in the body, they may cause the host to drink more alcohol or even to become an alcoholic. Consequently, anyone who goes to a bar, night club or any place where liquor is served or anyone who drinks alcohol or takes drugs increases the possibility of picking up discarnates, including discarnates who had serious addictions while in the body.

Automatic Writing and Ouija Boards

In other cases, I have found that people who do automatic writing or use Ouija boards may also leave themselves open for possession by discarnates. The object, of both automatic writing and Ouija boards, is to contact an advanced spirit who will work through them. The problem of working with an Ouija board or automatic writing is that most people do not know that they may simply pick up an earthbound discarnate who could be less advanced spiritually than they are. Unfortunately, once a person has opened themselves to discarnates, the discarnates take up residence and may be difficult to detect. My recommendation is to leave automatic writing and Ouija boards strictly alone. They should only be attempted by a person trained, skilled, and practiced in the art of self-protection through the use of light shields and positive prayer. When you begin to work with your High Self, you do not need a Ouija board.

I know a woman who started doing automatic writing. She was having a wonderful time communicating with a spirit and eagerly told everyone about her marvelous experience. Everything went great until the writing started telling her over and over again she was to commit suicide. She became very frightened and immediately stopped automatic writing. She had five discarnates which have now been sent into the light.

Hearing Voices

I have worked with several people who have heard voices and whose behavior was often very erratic, confused, and irrational. Because these people have heard voices, they have usually been diagnosed as schizophrenic. The problem is often entity possession and the voices are discarnates talking to them. The discarnates cause the host person to act in ways that are psychotic or schizoid in nature. Once the discarnates are cleared, the voices stop and the personality of the person makes an immediate change for the better, and that change is usually very dramatic. The actions that led to the diagnosis of schizophrenia are no longer displayed by the client.

Spirit Guides

The voices that people hear are not always from discarnates. Some are the voices of spirit guides or High Self working for the welfare of mankind. They channel information to Earth through mediums who are willing to work with them and who know how to protect themselves from discarnate invasion. "*A Course In Miracles*" and "The Seth Materials" are two examples of channeled writings.

An advanced spirit is a soul who has gone through the experience of many lifetimes, has grown to the point where they do not have to return for further lessons, and has gone on into the realms of light after leaving the physical plane. These souls may decide to reenter the earth level as a spirit guide to someone who is currently experiencing through a physical body. Every one who is in the earth level has at least one guide and most of the time there may be several guides working with an individual. When a person has made a conscious decision to walk a path of spiritual unfolding, more guides join them to assist in the work. These spirit guides are always benevolent and helpful although they can only help when the person is ready and then only to the degree that they are allowed. If you are interested in how many guides you have, simply use the pendulum and chart and ask for the number.

Discarnates Blocking Use of SRT

Many people who have discarnates are strong enough so that the system of Spiritual Re-sponse Therapy works without any difficulty. For others, the energy of the discarnates is sufficient to block use of the system. I have not kept an exact account of the number of people who have had discarnates which interfered with the work we were attempting to do. However, once I became aware that some people who were possessed still worked well with the system, I made some queries of my High Self. My High Self has a complete record of all the work that I have done with people through Spiritual Response Therapy, so I turned to it for some answers.

Q. *High Self, may I ask some questions concerning the people I have worked with and their possible possession by discarnates? (+)*

Q. *What percentage of the people with whom I have worked have I found discarnates in? (36%)*

Q. *What is the total percentage of people with whom I have worked, actually possessed by discarnates? (75%)*

Q. *Then I am leaving a lot of people with possessions that could be cleared? (+)*

Q. *Should I check each client to make certain that all of them who have discarnates are cleared? (+)*

My responsibility, as a Spiritual Response Therapist, is to do everything in my knowledge and power to help people free themselves from anything, past, present or future that is limiting their full and complete expression of life. Releasing discarnates is a major part of helping the person exercise their own power and dominion without the interference of discarnates.

Everyone on this planet could be helped by use of the releasing prayer given below even if they do not have discarnates. The prayer for filling yourself with light can be used before going out of the house to face the activities of the day. It can even be used to surround our homes with a shield of light for the protection of our property. I strongly suggest using the prayer for light, included in the releasing prayer, before going to a hospital or cemetery. No one needs the prayer if their energy field is high, but it is better to be safe and prayer has never hurt anyone.

Technique

It is my observation that you can never drive discarnates out using anger, hate, rage, or any discordant energy. They simply feed off the discordant energy and become more strongly entrenched. Patience, gentleness, prayer, talking them out, or asking High Self to remove them are the simplest and best ways. Many discarnates will exit if you can convince them that there is no criticism, judgment, condemnation, or punishment on the other side. Relatives who have stayed because they feel needed or who are addicted to a loved one need to be told that they are blocking their own spiritual progress as well as the progress of the loved one and, therefore, need to move on to the higher realms.

High Self will not clear discarnates when the person who acts as host has a strong desire to punish themselves and are using the discarnates to fulfill that desire. Every living soul has free agency and that free agency cannot be violated even by Spirit. Only when the person is ready to let go of the self-punishment program can Spirit clear them.

Never use your own energy to clear discarnates. Always work with Spirit (High Self). Let them do the work.

If you or a client seems to have a tendency to pick up discarnates, ask if you (or they) have programs causing this susceptibility. If so, research these programs as usual, then ask High Self to clear the programs.

Releasing Discarnates

Releasing discarnates is simple and easy. Just ask your High Self to remove them and they will. At other times, you may wish to use the following prayer. Sit quietly and proceed. (The prayer does not have to be in these exact words.)

There is but one Presence, Power and Mind. We are now one with the Presence, Power and Mind of God. We are filled with the light of Spirit. Every cell and fiber of our being is filled with the powerful white light of Spirit. This light dissolves all darkness and limitation and sets us free. The light vibrates at several thousand cycles per second and fills our minds and hearts. It now flows out to surround us with a shield of energy. Only the highest vibrations may now enter. We call on our guides to assist us at this time. We ask the masters of light to be with us as we release these discarnates. May the Holy Spirit guide and protect us and set us free.

We say to all of these discarnates: This is not your home. You do not have to stay in the earth vibrations. You are free to go into the light. There is no criticism, condemnation, judgment or punishment in the realms of light. Every desire can be fulfilled there and you can even create a new body for yourself. Turn and look around you. You will see a light. Move toward the light. As you do so, there will be angels of light, loved ones, or friends to take you by the hand and lead you on into the light. Reach out. Take their hands. Go into the light. You are free. We love you, bless you, and set you free. And we are free. Thank you, Father! Amen.

Once this process has been completed, I use the pendulum and ask my High Self the following questions:

Q. *How many discarnates do we have left? (pendulum swings to zero)*

Q. *Have they all gone into the their right and perfect place? (+)*

There are a limited number of cases when all of the discarnates have not gone into the light and the process must be repeated. When there is an indication that all of the discarnates have not left, you simply repeat the prayer again, assuring the remaining discarnates that there is no reason to fear going into the light. Sometimes the remaining discarnate is a relative who has made their transition and they want to be acknowledged as family and receive special treatment. They do not want to be treated as "just one more discarnate." At other times, the discarnate has committed murder and is fearful of punishment or more often of retaliation by the person they have killed. Interesting enough, it is easy to get them to move into the light by having them look into the light and see the very person they murdered waiting with open arms, assuring them that they are alive and well and hold no malice toward the person who murdered them.

Case study #1: Possession

I have worked with people who have brought discarnates in from past lives in other dimensions. These discarnates will not usually show up until we are working in the realm of past lives in other dimensions, but in Deborah's case, the discarnates from past lives in other dimensions influenced the entire clearing process.

We quickly established the movements of the pendulum, asked some check questions and started work. There was only one problem—it didn't work. There was only one block and it was from past lives in other dimensions. We made a lot of releasing statements in an attempt to remove the block and nothing worked. I finally asked High Self for permission to do the clearing work by my holding the pendulum. Each session began with an attempt to clear the block (without success) and proceeded with my holding the pendulum to do the work. Not until the fifth session was Deborah able to hold the pendulum and get logical answers. We finally found that the problem from past lives in other dimensions was discarnates. Now, when trying to find what the blocks are to working with the system, if discarnates in past lives is indicated, I simply ask my High Self to clear them.

Case study #2: Multiple personalities

Linda K. Green is a qualified document examiner and expert witness. She analyses handwriting and testifies in court cases. Linda first came to see me regarding two clients whose handwriting she had analyzed. Checking for entities, I found that the female client had one discarnate. The male client had six. Linda was fascinated by this because the woman had two forms of handwriting and the male had seven forms. She thought she was dealing with multiple personalities but suspected that there might be something else involved. She was right. They were not multiple personalities of the individuals. They were the personalities of each individual plus the personalities of the discarnates who had taken up residence.

Case study #3: Discordant energy on sister

Being able to work with your High Self to see if you or someone else has discarnates has a definite advantage because most people are not aware when there is possession. Emily was one of the few people who was. We were working to clear the discordant energy she had on a sister and the pendulum went to discarnates as the major reason for the problem. Through intuition, Emily was consciously aware that her sister was a host to discarnates but did not know how many she had. It is not always important to know the number of discarnates, but it is important to release them.

Case study #4: Possession

I had always been dubious regarding the possibility of people being possessed of evil spirits. Not that I did not believe it was possible, but I felt that most people tended to blow it all out of proportion. Too much fear and discordant emotions were combined with a desire to make possession a bizarre and sensational experience.

My first experience with discarnates resulted from a phone call to the church where I was a minister. Hilda, a woman in her twenties called and said her husband, Ralph, seemed to be possessed of an evil spirit and asked if my wife and I, as ministers, could help him. We made an appointment and went to their home. The discarnate had been talking to Ralph and telling him that he was going to kill him. Ralph had recently experienced several accidents that could have proven very serious. Several weeks before Hilda called, Ralph had attempted suicide.

After a discussion with the couple, we began a prayer process in which we exhorted the discarnate to leave the physical plane and go into the light.† It appeared that the discarnate did not want to leave and as we prayed, a struggle ensued between Ralph and the discarnate. Ralph's body would stiffen and jerk convulsively as the discarnate sought to maintain its grip on him. Finally, after considerable prayer, the discarnate was released and went into the light. Ralph was completely relaxed and stated that he felt better than he had in weeks.

We then went through all of the rooms in the house and used a prayer process to clear them of discordant energy and fill them with light. We told the couple to call us if there was any more trouble with discarnates and we would

---

†Since we learned to work with our High Self committees, we just ask High Self to clear the client of all discarnates and extra souls and to clear the building and grounds of all discordant energies and to fill all the geopathic zones with light.

clear the area again. We have not heard from them again so we assume that the discarnate did not return. Since that occasion, my whole awareness of possible interference or possession by discarnates has changed.

Case study #5: Discarnates in possession and in auric field

Nancy was a very loving and gentle person. She heard voices and thought it was God's way of talking to her. Unfortunately, the information was not always beneficial and would often cause her pain and difficulty. When we started Spiritual Response Therapy, she easily established the "yes" and "no" movements of the pendulum. I asked several check questions and then started working to clear a specific problem. Nothing worked. None of the answers we received made sense. It was my belief that the voices were a result of discarnate possession and they were interfering with the swing of the pendulum. Not being certain what was happening I called a friend, who was able to work with her High Self, and asked her to check what was going on with Nancy. She confirmed my suspicion of discarnate possession and we set up an appointment to work together and clear them. Note: This case came up before I had learned to work with my High Self.

There were eleven discarnates in all, three in possession and eight in Nancy's auric field. It only took a few minutes to clear all of the discarnates. The following week, when I worked with Nancy, she had picked up more discarnates and was hearing voices again. We went through another three minute process of sending them into the light. For the next several sessions, as we continued to work together, we had to clear her of discarnates before we could proceed with Spiritual Response Therapy. Since that time, she has called me several times and asked me to check for discarnates. Sometimes, working with my High Self, discarnates would be revealed and we would simply pray over the phone together and release them. At other times there were no entities. As I continued to work with Nancy, the time between de-possession and repossession increased. Nancy has been very faithful in working daily with a prayer which I gave her for creating a shield of white light around herself as a protection against discarnates.

There are many ways that a person can pick up discarnates in either the auric field or in body possession or in both. Nancy first became host to discarnates when she was under anesthesia during an operation. Later, she took prescription drugs which kept her auric vibrations low and discarnates could invade her space.

Case study #6: Possession by discarnates

Bob had discarnates and alcohol was suspected as the culprit. However, when we asked if the discarnates were a result of the alcoholism, a "no" response was received. When asked if it was because of drugs, a "yes" response was received. I asked Bob if he had ever used drugs and was informed that he had used marijuana once. Further questioning of the subconscious revealed that once was enough to open his aura and allow the possession by the discarnates.

Case study #7: Possession caused by drinking alcohol

Working with Tim (the real estate salesman mentioned in other chapters) was difficult because he had discarnates. Every time we released them and tried to accomplish productive work, we found he had picked up others. Again and again we cleared Tim of discarnates only to find he was hosting some new ones. We simply could not keep him clear enough to do any work on his personal programs. Finally, I asked permission of my High Self to hold the pendulum and find all of the information on the programs we were trying to clear on Tim. Permission was given and we proceeded with the counseling. I worked with Tim for several two hour sessions without keeping him clear of discarnates.

Several weeks later after many of his programs had been cleared he said to me, "You know I am an alcoholic, don't you?" That was the reason he kept picking up discarnates. Many of those he hosted had been addicted to alcohol while in the body and were helping Tim maintain his drinking so they could feed off his energy.

Case study #8: Possession

Abrupt personality changes may be an indication of possession. While working with Mabel, I found she had discarnates, which we released. During our discussion, I had mentioned that an abrupt personality change was often an indication of discarnate possession. She said that her niece had undergone a dramatic change in personality about two years ago and asked if I could check with my High Self and see if the niece was possessed. I said I would. Holding the pendulum, I asked the following questions:

Q. *Can I ask some questions in regard to Ruby? (+)*

Q. *Does Ruby have discarnates? (+)*

Q. *How many does she have? (six - using chart)*

I then tried to continue my work with Mabel to clear her programs but the system had stopped working. I made every possible check to identify the problem, had Mabel repeat some releasing statements to remove blocks, and nothing worked. After about ten minutes of frustration, Mabel said, "Robert, do you suppose it has something to do with the discarnates we found in Ruby?" Holding a pendulum, I asked:

Q. *Does the system not working have anything to do with the fact that we found discarnates in the niece? (+)*

Q. *Do we need to release them? (+)*

Having received permission to release the discarnates, we went through the prayer process and checked to make certain the discarnates had departed and the niece was clear.

Q. *How many discarnates does Ruby have now? (zero)*

Q. *Did they all go into the light? (+)*

When Mabel and I resumed work, we found no further problem with the system. Since I started providing Spiritual Response Therapy, Spirit has continued to teach me many lessons. This was just one more.

CHAPTER 22

Building Awareness
ℰ ℛ

We are wonderful creatures you and I. We are created in the image and likeness of God. There is the seed of unlimited greatness in every individual that is waiting eagerly to grow into its expanded potential and burst into full and glorious bloom. The growth of the individual can be greatly enhanced through the process of Spiritual Response Therapy.

My Process of Growth Through SRT

In a comparatively short time I have learned more about my fellow human beings and about myself than I ever dreamed possible. Working with the system has provided me with a greatly expanded understanding of how we design and orchestrate our own individual life expression and of the extremely intricate relationship we have with other people. I have watched clients become free from the past and change and grow in marvelous ways. I have also experienced greater personal growth and awareness than I ever believed I could accomplish in one lifetime.

However, it has not been without its measure of pain and frustration. There are some areas of life, such as predicting the future that are better left alone. Also, I have gotten into personal ego while trying to work with release counseling, and this has caused me considerable difficulty and pain.

> Not by might, nor by power, but by my spirit, saith the Lord of hosts. (Zechariah 4:6)

Ego! How quickly we can get caught up in our own ego self. But staying in the spirit of patience and wisdom keeps a person out of the ego and out of difficulty.

When I first started working with Response Therapy, it was under the instruction of Clark and Sharon Cameron. During training we worked on clearing the discordant energy I held on my father and mother, my blocks to my prosperity and a few other areas. After about six months of counseling other people, I discovered, to my surprise, the positive energy was one hundred percent and the discordant energy was zero on all significant people in my life except on God on whom I held fifty percent discordant energy.

Although I had not cleared discordant energy on my personal programs, they were clear. Obviously something had happened during the six months that had dramatically affected my own inner programs. I concluded that every time I gave a releasing statement to one of my clients, it altered my own subconscious programming. If there was any program in me that was similar to the program being released from the subconscious mind of the client, it was released the moment I gave the client the statement they were to repeat. Every releasing statement was clearing me, every positive statement I was giving to them was programming my subconscious mind in a positive way. Thus, the blessing that I had given to others through my Spiritual Response Therapy has blessed me beyond meas·re.

There is an often-repeated statement: "In blessing you are blessed, and in cursing you are cursed." The personal benefit I have received from Spiritual Response Therapy has been greater than that received by any of my clients. Working with others has been invaluable just for the benefits accrued in my own personal life. And, it is extremely satisfying to know that in the process of helping yourself you are blessing others.

The discordant energy I held on God involved nine past lives. In six of those lives, I died as a soldier. During the other three lives, I was a woman killed by soldiers. It was easy to clear the energy.

Caution #1

Let me give a word of caution. Trying to use the system by yourself, without the assistance of a trained counselor, may lead you into blind alleys, cause confusion and bring frustration and pain. Even after extensive training in the system, I find myself getting into situations that cause confusion. This is especially true when I try to take shortcuts and fail to follow the system in a logical, step-by-step process. When this happens, I go back to basics and start over with the questioning process.

Caution #2

Some people, after they have worked with a counselor, try to use the system to reveal the future. It simply does not work. Remember that the future is based on the grand total of all the thoughts that you hold in mind at the present moment and on the energies that you attach to those thoughts. In the church where I am an ordained minister, the basic concept is, "Thoughts held in mind, produce after their kind." I would like to add to that statement, "Thoughts held in mind, charged with the energy of your emotions, produce after their kind." Through the process of Spiritual Response Therapy, you have changed both the thoughts held in mind and the associated energies. Therefore, you have changed the basic programs that affect the current life expression, and even more so, the future.

You produce the future out of the wellspring of the subconscious mind energies through your conscious and unconscious decisions. Ralph Waldo Emerson would call this "the law of compensation." The Old Testament states, "As a man thinketh in his heart (thought and feeling); so is he" (Proverbs, 23:7). A basic premise in physics is, "for every action, there is a reaction." The emotional energies that you hold in your heart are constantly sending out into the world their constructive or destructive messages that produce your so-

called good or bad luck. Once a person is clear of their basic discordant programming, it prepares the ground of the subconscious mind to receive new, positive thoughts and energies that will bring a new crop of future good. By holding constructive thoughts and charging those thoughts with energy, you may design your own future according to your conscious desires. Change the inner pattern of thoughts and feelings and the future is automatically changed whether you want it to change or not.

Caution #3

Another word of caution—never use the power of your own thought and feelings to manipulate or pressure another person. That is spiritual trespass and can only lead to future pain and difficulty for you. Only what comes to the individual as a natural process of the universe unfolding is right and good.

I have also become aware that the desires you hold in the conscious mind may strongly affect the movements of the pendulum. If a person desires or believes strongly enough that they are to have an intimate relationship with a certain person, and they ask the subconscious mind if that is the right and perfect person for them, it will simply answer "yes. The conscious mind programmed the subconscious mind in the first place and is always in charge of determining what the person wants and receives. The subconscious always acquiesces to the desires of the conscious mind. No one has the right to force their will on another person. To do so is neither wise nor intelligent for it sets in motion a return energy that must be compensated for sooner or later.

Karma and Repeated Lifetimes

Karma, in my opinion (and High Self says this is true), is not a hard and fast rule of "an eye for an eye and a tooth for a tooth. It is rather, "That ye love one another, as I have loved you" (John 15:12), for what we hold in mind and charge with an energy, we create.

Working with one couple, I found that each had killed the other six or seven times in previous lives. They had been married about one year and were having a lot of problems in their relationship in the current life. I wanted to find out why they were back together in this life.

Was it because of unresolved thoughts and emotions?

Q. *Are you together in this life because of killing each other in past lives? (-)*

Q. *Are you together because of the unresolved energy established between you? (+)*

Q. *Are you together in this life to learn to honor and love each other? (+)*

I do not see repeated lifetimes as a form of punishment or to experience difficulties, as so many people do, rather, it is an opportunity for souls to get together and release the energy that has accumulated between them during past lives. The best and purest way to release that energy is through love. Love dissolves everything unlike itself and leaves only the pure essence of good. Your only purpose in life is to learn that you are created in the image and likeness of God and to express as nearly as possible that image and likeness of your Creator. "God is love, and he who abides in love abides in God, and God abides in him." (I John, 4:16)

Through the process of release counseling, clearer pictures are attained of how lifetime after lifetime we build the intricate fabric of life. I am fully convinced that not until mankind learns to live in peace and harmony with all people everywhere, will we have completed the Herculean task that has been placed before us. We, each, are individual players in the game of life, yet, we are all essential to the overall tapestry that is being woven in one life and re-woven again and again in subsequent lives. "He who overcomes, I will make him a pillar in the temple of my God, and he shall go no more forth." (Revelation, 3:12) When you have built your life on God (Love), you will not be required by the law of mind action to return to Earth or a similar level on another planet for further lessons. You will be established in the consciousness of Love and will not have to return.

Working with High Self

Being able to work with my High Self has been of fantastic benefit to both my clients and to myself. When working with my High Self, there are times when the answers are confused and a check reveals that I have encountered blocks or there is a charge on the program that I need to have High Self clear or I need to ask that the person's Guides, Guardian Angels, and High Self be cleared and harmonized.

While working with the High Self, I never assume that my contact is certain and permanent. From time to time I ask check questions to make sure I am still working with the High Self and getting correct answers. I ask Spirit to make certain that everything is still clear and to indicate on Chart 3 who I am working with. If High Self is not indicated, I know that there is something in the way.

Q. *Am I working with the High Self? (+)*

Q. *Will I receive correct answers? (+)*

Q. *Will I receive wrong answers? (-)*

Q. *Am I ready to start work? (+)*

Q. *CAN I ask some questions in regard to my client? (+)*

Q. *MAY I ask some questions in regard to her? (+)*

Q. *SHOULD I ask some questions in regard to her? (+)*

Q. *Are there any blocks or interference to using this system with her? (+)*

Q. *How many forms of interference are there? (Four, using chart with numbers)*

Q. *What is one of the forms? (discarnates in aura, Chart 1)*

Q. *How many discarnates are there? (eleven)*

Q. *What is another form? (discarnates in possession)*

Q. *How many discarnates are in possession? (five)*

Q. *What is the next form? (imprint)*

Q. *When was the imprint made? (Zero, using chart)*

Q. *Was it made at birth? (+)*

Q. *Is it an imprint of brain damage? (+)*

Q. *Is there more than one imprint? (-)*

Q. *What is the fourth form? (thought forms)*

Q. *Is there any other reason why the system will not work? (-)*

I then ask High Self to clear all these forms of interference and the system works beautifully.

Working with Clients

When I first worked with clients, I taught them how to use the pendulum and let them get the answer to the questions. Now, I ask the client if they would like me to do all of the necessary research of their programs, since as a result of my practice and experience, I have become very proficient and fast at working with High Self to find and clear the client's discordant programs.

The length of time it takes to work with a client and clear their problem areas varies greatly. A person's basic programs have been cleared in as little as a few minutes with a dramatic change taking place in their life. Others may take several hours to clear, and the changes may not be as dramatic.

Regardless of the amount of work accomplished with any client, there is never a time when Spiritual Response Therapy is no longer needed or without value to them. Like going to a doctor for a regular check-up in order to maintain perfect physical health, so too, Spiritual Response Therapy may be used as a means of checking the ongoing state of a person's mental and emotional health. One client comes to see me about once a month just to check up and clear anything that has come to her awareness since the last session. Every person may continue to work on their own with the releasing statements or with their High Self committee after completing Spiritual Response Therapy and will find great benefit in doing so.

Much of my work is now for clients who live in other parts of the world. They call me on the recommendation of a friend who has had the clearing work done and witnessed the wonderful changes that occurred in their own life. Working with High Self, I ask how long it will take to clear the caller's programs based on the information received over the phone. The caller is informed of the time and charges involved and arrangements for payment are made. It is my practice to get a credit card number or a check in hand before the work is started as some people do not fulfill their promises to pay.

Sometimes I am asked to clear a person free of charge because they are out of work and do not have the means of paying. I simply ask High Self if what they are telling me is correct. If High Self says it is correct and that the work should be done free of charge, I do it and send the work to the person with my blessings. There is a law of circulation in the universe, and it is important to observe that law. Jesus said to give and it would be given to you. Unfortunately, some people are takers only and never understand that it is necessary to give in order to receive. Therefore, they remain in poverty and the clearing work done for them has little value or effect on their life. However, it is not my responsibility to judge, so if Spirit says they want to clear them, I do the work.

Appendix A.

Charts

Blocks & Interference
© Detzler

Chart 1

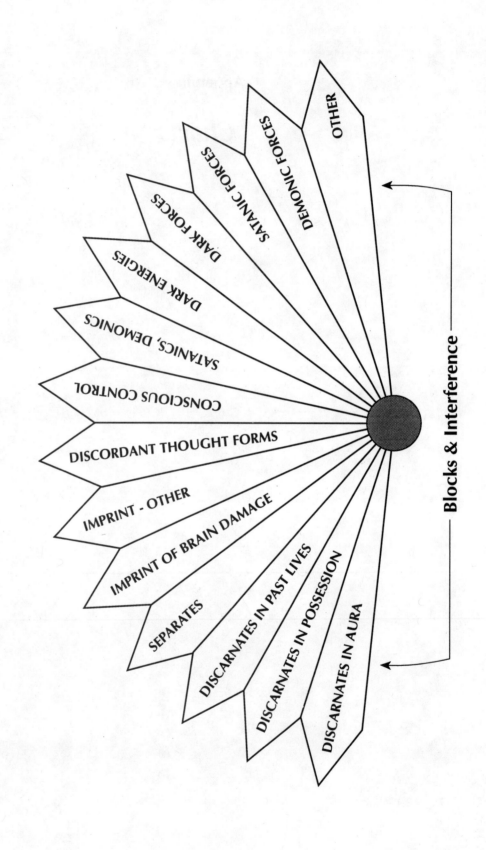

Blocks & Interference

OTHER

DEMONIC FORCES

SATANIC FORCES

DARK FORCES

DARK ENERGIES

SATANICS, DEMONICS

CONSCIOUS CONTROL

DISCORDANT THOUGHT FORMS

IMPRINT - OTHER

IMPRINT OF BRAIN DAMAGE

SEPARATES

DISCARNATES IN PAST LIVES

DISCARNATES IN POSSESSION

DISCARNATES IN AURA

Programs
When
© *Detzler*

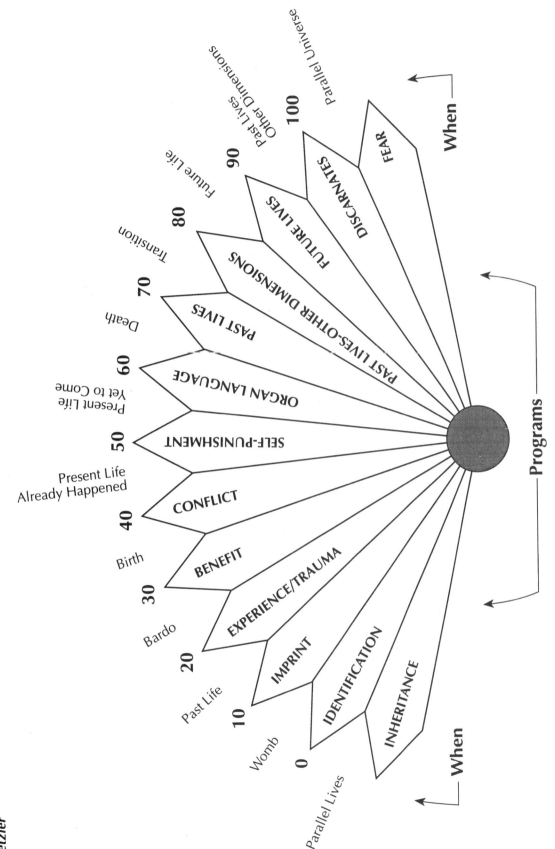

Chart 2

Cast of Characters
© Detzler

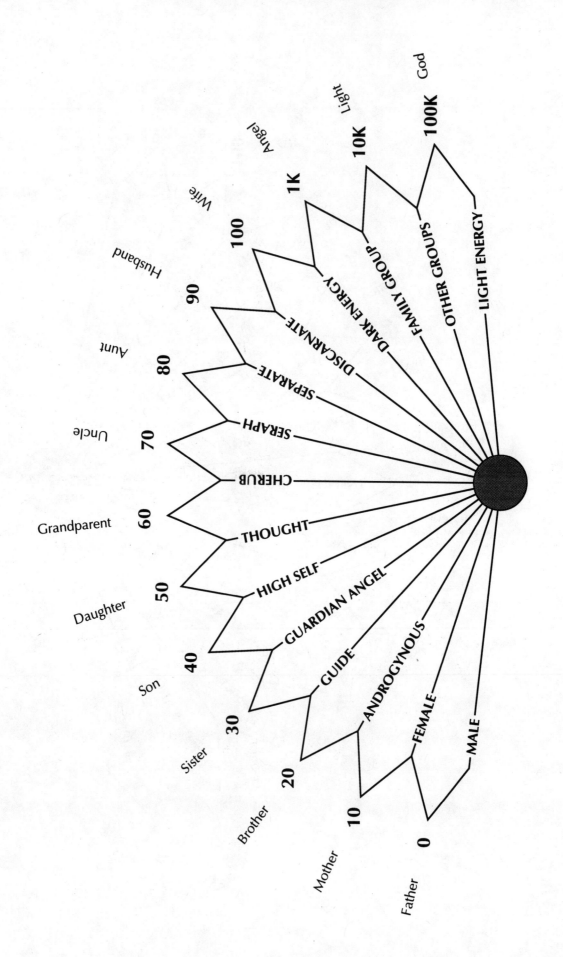

Chart 3

Discordant Energy

© Detzler

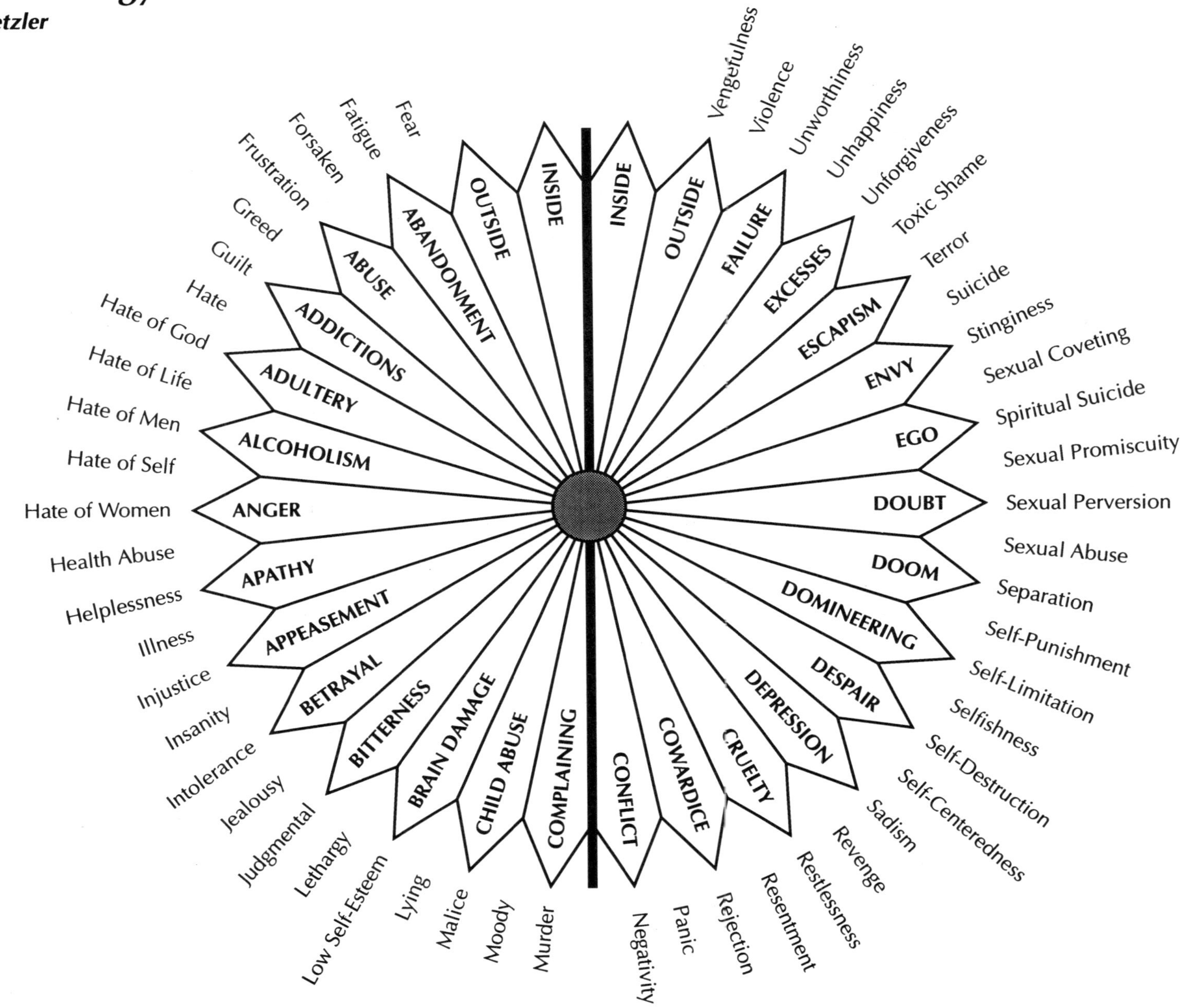

Chart 4

A circular radial chart titled "Discordant Energy." The petals radiating from a central hub are labeled (clockwise from top): EGO, DOUBT, DOOM, DOMINEERING, DESPAIR, DEPRESSION, CRUELTY, COWARDICE, CONFLICT, COMPLAINING, CHILD ABUSE, BRAIN DAMAGE, BITTERNESS, BETRAYAL, APPEASEMENT, APATHY, ANGER, ALCOHOLISM, ADULTERY, ADDICTIONS, ABUSE, ABANDONMENT, OUTSIDE, INSIDE, INSIDE, OUTSIDE, FAILURE, EXCESSES, ESCAPISM, ENVY.

Outer labels include: Sexual Coveting, Spiritual Suicide, Sexual Promiscuity, Sexual Perversion, Sexual Abuse, Separation, Self-Punishment, Self-Limitation, Selfishness, Self-Destruction, Self-Centeredness, Sadism, Revenge, Restlessness, Resentment, Rejection, Panic, Negativity, Murder, Moody, Malice, Lying, Low Self-Esteem, Lethargy, Judgmental, Jealousy, Insanity, Intolerance, Injustice, Illness, Helplessness, Health Abuse, Hate of Women, Hate of Self, Hate of Men, Hate of Life, Hate of God, Hate, Guilt, Greed, Frustration, Forsaken, Fatigue, Fear, Vengefulness, Violence, Unworthiness, Unhappiness, Unforgiveness, Toxic Shame, Terror, Suicide, Stinginess.

Worksheet

Name: _____ Date: _____

Address: _____ Phone: _____

City: _____ State: _____ Zip: _____ Work: _____

Referred by: _____

CHECK COUNSELING AREAS BELOW	Positive		Negative		Date Cleared
_____ Mother _____	_____	%	_____	%	_____
_____ Father _____	_____	%	_____	%	_____
_____ Stepmother _____	_____	%	_____	%	_____
_____ Stepfather _____	_____	%	_____	%	_____
_____ Mother substitute/s _____	_____	%	_____	%	_____
_____ Father substitute/s _____	_____	%	_____	%	_____
_____ Biological parents' relationship _____	_____	%	_____	%	_____
_____ Step relationship/s _____	_____	%	_____	%	_____
_____ Other important family members you grew up with, including siblings					
_____	_____	%	_____	%	_____
_____	_____	%	_____	%	_____
_____	_____	%	_____	%	_____
_____ Your spouse or mate _____	_____	%	_____	%	_____
_____ Your children _____	_____	%	_____	%	_____
_____	_____	%	_____	%	_____
_____	_____	%	_____	%	_____
_____	_____	%	_____	%	_____
_____	_____	%	_____	%	_____
_____	_____	%	_____	%	_____
_____	_____	%	_____	%	_____
_____ Your "ex's" _____	_____	%	_____	%	_____
_____ Yourself _____	_____	%	_____	%	_____
_____ God (whatever your concept is) _____	_____	%	_____	%	_____
_____ Life (whatever you are experiencing) _____	_____	%	_____	%	_____
_____ Other important person on whom you hold negative energy					
_____	_____	%	_____	%	_____
_____	_____	%	_____	%	_____
_____	_____	%	_____	%	_____
_____	_____	%	_____	%	_____
_____	_____	%	_____	%	_____

Major Aspects Of Life

Check Counseling Areas Below

_____ Birth (trauma)

_____ Close relationships

_____ Sex

_____ Marriage

_____ Divorce

_____ Children

_____ Learning

_____ Success

_____ Prosperity

_____ Health

_____ Exercise

_____ Diet

_____ Death

_____ Anger

_____ Guilt

_____ Grief (grieving)

_____ Self-punishment

_____ Self-esteem

_____ Work

_____ Failure

Appendix C.

SRT Procedure

The SRT Procedure

A. Clearing to Work

Do I have any blocks or interference?

Do I have any program or energy blocks?

Am I working with my High Self?
   Using Chart 3: Ask, "Please show me who I am working with."

Will I get correct answers?

Can I start work now?

B. Steps in Research (90% of all research is past life research.)

1. Is there a program to research?

2. What is the program? (Use Chart 2.)

3. When was it established? (Use Chart 2.)

4. Find the cast of characters (only major participants). Use Chart 3. List across the page. For past life research, find out who the client was, and then, who the remaining cast members were. For present life research, just find out who the other cast members are.

Example:	Client	Other	Other	Other	Other
	Female	Husband	Son	Daughter	Etc.

5. Was there hurt or harm?

6. Who was harmed? By whom?

7. Was it mental, emotional or physical harm?

8. Was it simple, serious or death?
    (Mental or emotional harm can be early death or suicide.)

9. If there wasn't any harm, ask whose energy needs to be cleared. Then use Chart 4 to find the energies.

10. Ask "Is this enough information to clear the program."
    If the program cannot be cleared, you may need to research one or more of the following items:
    *   Someone else's discordant energy
    *   One, or more, additional lives
    *   Find the ages of the cast
    *   Find who one or more of the cast is in this life

    When researching parallel lives, ask: "Is this enough information to clear the program? ... the life? ... the set of parallel lives?" You may need to research more lives to clear the program and/or the set of parallel lives.

11. Ask High Self to please clear all lives. (When researching parallel lives, be sure to ask High Self to clear and block all parallel lives between each other and between the parallel lives and this life, so that they can't bleed through.)

Appendix D.

Index of Case Studies

Appendix E.

Glossary

Akashic record: The record of everything the soul (Spiritual Body/living soul) has experienced from the instant of the Divine Blueprint formed at the level of the GODHEAD until the present moment and beyond. Another name is soul record.

Androgynous: Of neutral gender, used to describe the physical body type of beings in other dimensions. Depending on the planet where the past life was experienced, "androgynous" may mean the body form is (1) both male and female; or, (2) neither male nor female. At other times, High Self indicates androgynous when the male/female aspects of the soul do not split and they are incarnated in one body. Additionally, there are times when High Self says the body form is both male/female; but when I ask if they are androgynous, High Self gives me a negative response.

Angel: From the Greek, meaning "a messenger," or "a messenger of God." Angels are spiritual beings that can be from many levels of consciousness and have many functions.

Bardo: A Tibetan term meaning "between lives." When a soul is ready to incarnate for its next lessons, it stands in the Bardo and communicates with its High Self. The soul reviews its akashic (soul) record and determines what needs to be worked on during the next incarnation.

Cherub or Cherubim: According to the *Metaphysical Bible Dictionary*, "Cherubim of 1 Kings 8:6-8 were symbolic figures representing the attributes and majesty of God." They stand for unlimited, unfettered truths of being. They are also souls who hold an angel office or level of consciousness. They may serve as guide, Guardian Angel or High Self. When Cherub is indicated, I always ask if they are serving in an office. If a "yes" response is given, I ask what the office is: guide, Guardian Angel or High Self. Cherub is also one of the first forms of consciousness we take prior to our first incarnation.

Conscious mind: There are two forms: first, the conscious mind of the Spiritual Body is the living soul (Genesis 2:7, K.J.V.); second, there is a conscious mind that functions as part of the human expression. Through the five senses, it is the observer, decision-maker, and the programmer of the subconscious mind. The conscious mind does have storage capabilities and sometimes holds discordant beliefs even after programs are cleared from the subconscious. When you are searching for a reason why something has not changed, there may be a special area of the conscious mind that needs cleaning out, much like a closet under the stairs that is seldom used or entered. The conscious mind can have compartments (up to eighty-nine) which can hold specific messages that can restrict a person's greater expression of life.

Contracts: A soul that incarnates for a second round of incarnations and convinces others to incarnate with them may have contracts to pick up the other souls' programs. Another form of contract has to do with decaying universes, where a soul has a contract to pick up the discordant energy of the young souls living in the decaying universe, so the souls in that universe can be taken out and placed in an expanding universe.

Dark energy: The soul is created of the substance of Spirit, or Light, and dwells in Spirit/Light. When the soul decides to incarnate, it may have the sense that it left the realms of Light and became dark energy—that it took upon itself the belief in good (light) and evil (darkness). Spirit may also indicate that a person has dark energy when the person is caught up in any of the energies listed on Chart 4. These energies "blank out" the person's spiritual Light.

Dark energies can also be discarnates with discordant energy that they carried with them when they left the physical body. The energies can be comprised of (but not limited to) any or all of the items on Chart 4. All dark energies can be cleared by High Self.

Dark forces: Beings, either in or out of the body, who carry a lot of dark energy such as hate, anger, and so on (anything listed on Chart 4). They band together and may cause problems.

Death: A belief that, when we leave the physical body, we die. In truth, death (annihilation) does not exist—there is only change.

Demonic: Any soul who has left the physical body and carries with it a lot of bad energy. Demonics can often be murderers, rapists, drug traffickers, and so on. Demonic energy is worse than that of satanics.

Demonic forces: A group of souls who have left the physical body, and are earth bound. They have not left the physical realm for one reason or another. They carry bad energy and have banded together, usually with the purpose of causing problems for incarnated souls. They are vindictive and destructive. However, demonic forces cannot harm anyone unless that person allows it. For example, when a person has a program of self-punishment, he may open himself to discarnates of various temperament in order to fulfill that program. The energy of demonic forces is worse than that of satanic forces.

Devil: The aggregate of discordant thoughts and beliefs that have been built up in race consciousness through many generations of earthly experiences. The devil is simply an archetypal representation of the carnal mind which opposes and rejects God or Truth.

Discarnate: A soul who has left the physical body, but has not left the vibrations of the physical realm within 90 hours of exiting the body. Discarnates become earth-bound and cannot leave without help. Just ask High Self to remove them and take them into their right and perfect place.

Discarnates in aura: Discarnates may enter a person's auric field because the field may have holes in it caused by drugs, alcohol, anger, or other discordant energy; or, the auric field may be weak because it is vibrating at a low frequency. If the field vibrates at a rate under 800 cycles per second, the person may be open to discarnates. Ask the High Self to raise and keep the vibration at several thousand cycles per second, and heal any holes in the aura.

Discarnates in possession: Discarnates who have entered the vibrations of the physical, emotional, mental, etheric, or astral body.

Discarnates from past lives: When a person is hypnotically regressed to a past life, they encounter all of the energy of the past life and relive the whole experience. While working with SRT, you actually open the past life to the present time, although you do not usually re-experience the pain and trauma of the past life. However, if there were discarnates attached to the past life, they can come into the present time and be felt. Just ask High Self to remove them and take them to their right and perfect place.

Discordant energy: Any energy that is not completely positive in nature. For instance, all of the items on Chart 4 would be considered discordant. It is not what happens to the soul at any point in the experiential process that causes something to come back and create problems, it is the attached discordant energy that carries over from lifetime to lifetime.

Future lives: Future lives are simply an alternate reality, or dream state, in which you face and work through situations that you either need or want to work on for soul growth, but do not want to experience in the current life. Future lives are being lived now, and they will be completed before you leave this physical body.

God: As a designation for soul level, God represents any soul that has reached a level of soul consciousness high enough to serve as the God of a planet. The God of each planet is called "I AM THAT I AM." Moses was provided this name by God while on Mount Horeb (Exodus 3:13-15). This is the only instance in the Scriptures where the God of the planet actually names itself.

Guardian Angel: A being that is assigned to guard and protect an incarnated soul. Guardian Angels cannot act against the will of the individual they are to protect, and have greater ability to help when the individual asks. They can be found at many levels of spiritual consciousness. An incarnated being may have from one to an infinite number of Guardian Angels.

Guide: When a soul is out of the body and in spirit form, it can serve as someone's guide. Under certain circumstances, a soul can also serve as a guide while still in the body if his or her soul consciousness is high enough. The higher the guide's level of soul consciousness, the purer the soul and the better they are able to guide and help.

High Self: Jesus referred to His High Self as The Father Within. High Self is the master teacher within. Everyone has a High Self which may consist of from one to an infinite number of souls.

Ideomotor response: A muscle movement that is initiated by our thoughts as a result of a programmed response. Example: Once the body has been trained to run, all a person has to do is think run and the muscles respond.

Imprint: A belief that is imprinted upon the subconscious mind during an emotionally charged time. The imprint can be given to you by yourself or by someone else. For example, perhaps you were born during the depression of the late 20's and early 30's, and your grandmother said to your parents, "You shouldn't have a child. You can't afford it. How will you ever provide for it in these trying times?" As a result of this conversation, you may have given yourself an imprint that you should not have been born because you were a financial burden on your parents.

Imprint of brain damage: An imprint, often registered at birth, to the effect that the person sustained brain damage. The doctor may have used forceps in the delivery process and thought, "I hope I do not damage this child's brain." The soul may have understood this as actual brain damage, and later expressed life as though there was actual brain damage. Seldom is there actual brain damage.

Imprint other: This is usually an imprint of brain damage as a result of disease (Alzheimer's, Down's Syndrome, and so on), statements by others, a head injury, or messages of insanity in past lives. Some people were accused of insanity in past lives and were incarcerated in an institution. High Self says that most of the time, they were not insane.

Jehovah: This is one of the names for the Christ, the Son of God. Jehovah symbolizes the perfect expression of the GODHEAD expressing itself as all life, substance, and intelligence. When mankind has developed his creative nature through the process called incarnation, and has returned to the consciousness of Spirit with full awareness he is the Jehovah, the Christed one, the Son of God.

Karmic beliefs: Karma is a belief system like the Old Testament teachings of an "eye for an eye and a tooth for a tooth." In Hinduism and Buddhism, karma is the belief that what you have done in previous lives, good and bad, will bring a reward or punishment in the current life. Karma is based on the belief that we must suffer for our misdeeds, rather than realizing that all experiences are simply steps in our growth. High Self informs me that the only karma is love. Negative karma is simply the beliefs that we set up when we partook of the tree of the knowledge of good and evil and incarnated.

Light: The essence of God as the highest form of creative substance. This is the very ground of our being as symbolized in Genesis 2:7.

Light energy: God is Light and we are created of this Light as Spiritual Bodies/living souls. Thus, when Jesus said, "You are the light of the world. . . . Let your light so shine . . ." (Matthew 5:14, 16), He was speaking of the truth of our very being. Our goal is to regain the knowledge that we are indeed Light of the ONE Light, and magnify it in all that we do.

Parallel lives: An incarnation that is being lived at the same time you are living the present one. A parallel life can be lived on this planet or another planet; in this galaxy or in another galaxy. The number of parallel lives a person can be living may be from a single life to many thousands. A person can be living parallel lives in several different galaxies at the same time.

Parallel universe: A universe parallel to this one, but invisible to us because it is vibrating at a different frequency. Each life lived in a parallel universe can have a record of past lives that were lived within that universe, as well as past lives in other dimensions.

Past lives: Any life in a physical body lived anywhere in the universe. It is still considered a past life if the soul is out of the body and serving as a guide, Guardian Angel, High Self or in some other capacity. When you have picked up the essence of another soul, their past lives register as part of your total number of past lives.

Past lives in other dimensions: Past lives that have not been experienced as an incarnation on planet Earth. They may be at other vibratory levels or dimensions. They could also be in the spiritual dimensions where you are serving as a guide, Guardian Angel, High Self, or in some other capacity.

Pendulum: Any object attached to a string or chain that can be moved easily by the muscles through an ideomotor response. There is no particular advantage of one type of pendulum over another except for the persons's own preference or belief.

Program: A program is a belief that has been accumulated in the soul records as a result of experiences before the soul incarnates, while the soul is incarnated, and between lives while the soul is in the spiritual realms.

Satan: Any soul whose power is derived through the unlawful use and expression of their spiritual potential and abilities.

Satanic forces: A group of discarnates with bad energies that have banded together.

Satanics: Discarnates with bad energies. Just as there are people who have different degrees of good and bad energy, so there are discarnates who have different degrees of good and bad energy that they carry with them when they leave the physical body. (See also *Demonics* and *Discarnates*.)

Savior: Savior is a spiritual path that I call "the greased pole," because it is the most difficult path to follow. The requirements are stringent and demanding and often difficult to accomplish. The Savior path is made up of two levels of Savior, first and second. There is one second-level Savior for each planet in the universe, but there may be many first-level saviors. A first-level savior is any spiritual teacher who comes to bring greater knowledge and wisdom. First-level saviors may be teachers, writers, healers, and so on. There are many on Earth, and they are under the direction of Jesus, who is the second-level Savior of this beautiful planet. A person can serve as first-level savior on one planet and still be a second-level Savior on another planet, since the soul and its expressions are without limit.

Separates: Beings who do not want to work within one of the seventy offices in a category spirit calls Ones. They enter the earth vibrations and independently try to help people. Unfortunately, they do not help and actually may cause problems because their high vibrations interfere with the incarnated person's vibrations. They must not stay in the earth vibrations for more than forty-two days or they become stuck. Once this happens, they need help to leave. Other separates deliberately enter the earth realms and attach themselves to people who are using Spiritual Response Therapy, as they want to have their programs cleared.

Seraph or Seraphim: Heavenly Beings that Isaiah saw in his vision, described in the sixth chapter of Isaiah. They represent wholeness or completeness, ideas of purity or the cleansing power of spiritual ideas. Seraph is often indicated as the form of the soul before first incarnation. Seraphim may serve as guides, Guardian Angels, High Self, and other offices at countless levels throughout the spiritual realms.

Spirit: Any being in the spiritual realms who is of a high enough consciousness to have access to an incarnated person's soul records and who can assist that person in accessing and clearing those records of discordant energy. Any soul that is assigned to an incarnated being to help them in their daily process of life. Each person has three standing committees of spiritual beings. They are called guides, Guardian Angels and High Self. These spirit beings are limited in their ability to help the individual until the person learns to contact and work with them, asking for what guidance they need to live a better life.

Spiritual Response Therapy (SRT): A spiritual process of working with your spiritual committee to access soul records, discover the discordant energy involved, and have that energy cleared by the spiritual committee and replaced with positive energy.

Subconscious mind: There are two forms. The first form is the subconscious mind of the Spiritual Body. This is where all the wisdom and knowledge that is gained on the soul path is stored; it is the repository for the akashic record. The second form is that of the human expression. This is where all of the incarnational experiences are recorded and stored. Those records, along with the akashic record, which is programmed into the cellular memory of the physical body immediately after birth, determine the process and quality of the soul's life. The information picked up as a result of the incarnational process is stored in the subconscious mind until the soul leaves the body. Only then are the records transferred to the akashic record repository.

Thought: Thought is the first form of manifestation and starts at the GODHEAD long before physical expression. Also, a soul may be identified as "thought" when it is planning to incarnate for the second round to work on its master programs. Thought, in this case, is what the soul is holding in consciousness as the curriculum for its second round of incarnations. Thought can also be indicated when the person's consciousness is filled with bitter or dysfunctional thoughts, such as anger, bitterness, fear, hate, or unforgiveness.

Transition: A major change in consciousness. Spirit has given three examples: transition brought about by moving from one environment to another, leaving the physical body in death or one soul leaving the body and another entering.

Tree: An archetypal representation of any structure of consciousness that has life and is added to in the process of experiencing, learning, and growing. A tree may be formed of good only or it may be a mixture of good and evil. It is always the soul's choice what tree (knowledge) it will partake of. The trees in the Garden of Eden represent structures of consciousness, or living beliefs within the consciousness of God. We partake of different trees (beliefs) of consciousness lifetime after lifetime as our soul learns and grows. It is best to look at the experiences of life as lessons to be encountered and knowledge to be gained. We separate the wheat (positive energy) from the chaff (discordant energy) and eat of only the highest order of trees (beliefs).

Yahweh (Hebrew): The self-existent One that reveals itself to Its creation, through Its creation, as Its creation; Elohim, God over the Super Super Universe. Yahweh at the GODHEAD is all life, substance, and intelligence seeking to express itself. Yahweh, at the level of I AM, is the extension of all life, substance, and intelligence as the spiritual realms.

Appendix F

Releasing Statements, Affirmations and Prayers

Chapter 3. The System

I now release all belief, perception and judgment that my Mother and Father did not provide sufficient emotional and financial support while I was growing up.

I now release all need and desire to belive that my Mother and Father did not provide sufficient emotional and financial support while I was growing up.

I now completely accept and believe and I instruct my subconscious mind to completely accept and believe on every level of my being that my parents did provide me with sufficient emotional and financial support while I was growing up...They loved me and supported me in every way...There is only God. Therefore, there is only love. Therefore, my parents loved me and I love my parents.

I release all belief, perception and judgment that it was a dumb, stupid thing to leave the realms of Light and incarnate.

I release all need and desire to believe that it was a dumb, stupid thing to leave the realms of Light and incarnate.

I now completely accept and believe and I instruct my subconscious mind to completely accept and believe on every level of my being that it was a wise and wonderful thing I did when I chose to incarnate for I have gained knowledge, wisdom, and stature in the sight of God.

Chapter 8. Removing Blocks and Interference

I release my belief, perception and judgment that the doctor (nurse, parent, or other) said I have brain damage. I release all need or desire to believe that I have brain damage. I release all need or desire to believe anything but that my brain is perfect and functions with one hundred percent accuracy. I am wise and intelli-gent. I learn quickly and easily and have a marvelous ability to retain and to instantly recall all that I have seen, read and experienced.

I release my belief, perception and judgment that there are any thought forms blocking the use of this system of counseling. I release all need and desire to have any thought forms block me from using this system. I release all need and desire to believe that there are any discordant thought forms blocking me now. I release all need and desire to believe anything but that all discordant thought forms are now dissolved and that this system works perfectly.

I release all fear of answering the question. I release all resistance to answering the question. I release all fear of working with the subconscious mind. I give the subconscious mind permission to answer the question.

Chapter 10. Identification

I release my belief, perception, and judgment that my father/mother did not hold me, hug me, and love me every day until I was five. I release my belief, perception, and judgment that my father/mother did not hold me, hug me, and love me every day until I was ten. I release my belief, perception, and judgment that my father/mother did not hold me, hug me, and love me every day until I was fifteen. I release my belief, perception, and judgment that my father/mother did not hold me, hug me and tell me how much they loved me every day until I was twenty. I release my belief, perception, and judgment that my father/mother has not held me, hugged me, and told me how much they admire and appreciate me every day of my life. I release my belief, perception, and judgment that my father/mother is not with me now any time I need them to hold me, hug me, and tell me how great and wonderful I am and how much they love me.

I release my beliefs, perceptions, and judgments, and my needs and desires to believe that my father is thoughtless.

I release all belief, perception and judgement that my father is thoughtless, selfish, belligerant, and self-centered.

I now completely accept and believe and instruct my subconscious mind to completely accept and believe on every level of my being that my father is loving, kind, thoughtful, considerate and always has my highest and best interest at heart.

I release all my beliefs, perceptions and judgments that I am thoughtless. I release all my needs and desires to believe I am thoughtless. I now completely accept and believe and instruct my subconscious mind to completely accept and believe on every level of my being that I am kind, thoughtful, loving, wise, orderly, constructive, peaceful, joyful, happy, and I always express my life in a positive way.

Chapter 12. Experience/Trauma

I release all fear of answering the question. I release all resistance to the answer. I give the subconscious permission to answer the question.

There is no judgment, criticism, condemnation, or punishment. There is only a desire to know the truth and to be free. Answer the question.

Chapter 14. Conflict

I release my belief, perception and judgment that Bill is too pure for me.

Chapter 10. Self-Punishment

Due to its length, the "Clearing the Files Meditation" is not repeated here.

Chapter 17. Past Lives In Other Dimensions

I release my belief, perception and judgment that because I was a great speaker or debater in a previous life I must argue on the school grounds now. I release all need or desire to argue on the school grounds now. I release all need and desire to believe anything but I am free from arguing on the school grounds now. However, I may use my talents as an orator, as I grow up, to become a great speaker in my chosen profession.

Chapter 21. Discarnates

There is but one Presence, Power and Mind. We are now one with the Presence, Power and Mind of God. We are filled with the light of Spirit. Every cell and fiber of our being is filled with the powerful white light of Spirit. This light dissolves all darkness and limitation and sets us free. The light vibrates at several thousand cycles per second and fills our minds and hearts. It now flows out to surround us with a shield of energy. Only the highest vibrations may now enter. We call on our guides to assist us at this time. We ask the masters of light to be with us as we release these discarnates. May the Holy Spirit guide and protect us and set us free.

We say to all of these discarnates: This is not your home. You do not have to stay in the earth vibrations. You are free to go into the light. There is no criticism, condemnation, judgment or punishment in the realms of light. Every desire can be fulfilled there and you can even create a new body for yourself. Turn and look around you. You will see a light. Move toward the light. As you do so, there will be angels of light, loved ones, or friends to take you by the hand and lead you on into the light. Reach out. Take their hands. Go into the light. You are free. We love you, bless you, and set you free. And we are free. Thank you Father! Amen.

Contract with High Self

1. For a "yes" answer, the pendulum is moved in a forward and back motion. For a "no" answer, the pendulum is moved in a side to side motion. A small circular movement indicates you are in neutral or that the question I have asked was not asked in such a way that it can be answered. A large circular motion indicates that you are clearing.

2. When researching the cast of characters, you will require only the major characters and if members of a family are involved, you will indicate "family group" instead of each individual relative. If it is necessary to single out a specific family member, you will do so.

3. If I must stop doing research before it is completed, you will automatically close the record until I can return to the work.

4. When I ask "Do I have any blocks?" or if I substitute the words "programs," "discordant energies," or "issues," for the word "blocks," you will check for any blocks, issues, programs, reasons, beliefs, perceptions, judgments, thoughts, feelings, discordant energies, interference, fears, contracts.

5. Whenever I pick up the pendulum to get answers, you will automatically clear me, my work space and the person for whom I am working and erect a shield so that I will not be disturbed. When you are ready for me to ask questions, you will move the pendulum in a "yes" response; but if I have interference or am not in neutral, you will indicate that by moving in a "no" response.

6. If contracts are indicated, you will automatically have them completed.

Continued on next page

7. During research, you will use these positions on the chart to mean the following:

Person Indicated or Question	Left Corner	Middle	Right Corner
Father	Head Monk	Biological	High Priest
Mother	Mother Superior	Biological	High Priestess
Brother	Monk	Biological	Priest
Sister	Nun	Biological	Priestess
Son	Student	Child	Priest
Daughter	Student	Child	Nun
Grandparent	Authority figure	Biological	Religious Leader/Pope
Office Held?	Guide	Guardian Angel	High Self
Was there harm?	Simple	Serious	Death
Type of harm?	Mental	Emotional	Physical
Type of death?	Burned or Burned & Tortured	Stoned	Crucified
Activity?	Teaching	Healing	Channeling
Type of Channeling?	Information	Both	Healing
Type of Healing?	Laying on of Hands	Both	Herbal/Natural
More info needed?	Age	Energy on Chart 4	Who they are now
Info received from?	High Self/Godhead	Other	Self
Which of 2 options	1st option stated	Both	2nd option stated
Which of 3 options	1st option stated	2nd option stated	3rd option stated
Number of digits	Tens	Hundreds	Thousands or More
Fear or Shame is?	Specific	Both	General

Bibliography

1. *Cheek, David B., M.D., and LeCron, Leslie M., B.A.* Clinical Hypnotherapy *(Orlando: Grune and Stratton, A subsidiary of Harcourt Brace Javanovich, 1968).*

2. *Detzler, Robert E..* Soul Re-Creation. *(Redmond, SRC Publishing, 1994).*

3. *Fiore, Edith, PhD.* The Unquiet Dead *(New York, Doubleday, 1987).*

4. The Holy Bible, King James Version. *(Nashville, Thomas Nelson, Inc., 1976).*

5. *LeCron, Leslie M.,* Techniques of Hypnotherapy *(New York: Julian Press, 1961).*

6. *LeCron, Leslie M.,* Self Hypnotism: the Technique and Its Use in Daily Living *(Englewood Cliffs, NJ: Prentice-Hall, Inc., 1964).*

7. *Pecci, Ernest F.,* I Love You/I Hate You. *(Pleasant Hill, IIT Publications, 1975).*

8. *Roberts, Jane.* The Nature of Personal Reality *(New York: Prentice-Hall Press, 1974). This is a Seth book.*

9. *Thompkins, Peter and Bird, Christopher.* The Secret Life of Plants *(New York: Harper & Row, 1973).*

10. *Whitton, Joel and Fisher, Joe.* Life Between Life *(New York, Doubleday, 1986).*

11. *Winn, Ralph B., PhD.* Dictionary of Hypnosis *(New York: Philosophical Library, 1965).*

Index